THE PLAYMAKER'S DECISIONS

THE SCIENCE OF CLUTCH PLAYS, MENTAL MISTAKES AND ATHLETE COGNITION

DANIEL PETERSON
LEONARD ZAICHKOWSKY, PHD

First published in the United States of America by Intelligens Press
LLC, 2020

Book cover design by Adrijus Guscia

CONTENTS

INTRODUCTION

"Good decisions come from experience. Experience comes from making bad decisions." -Mark Twain

---

A s the confetti floated down from the top of Mercedes-Benz Stadium in Atlanta, Nick Saban stopped Tom Rinaldi in his tracks. The veteran ESPN reporter had his opening question queued until the Alabama football head coach patted his chest with a wry grin to declare, "I'm asking the questions." Rinaldi yielded the microphone, to which Saban asked an obvious, rhetorical question, "Was that a good game or what?" Saban and his Crimson Tide had just walked off with the 2018 College Football Playoff national championship in an

DANIEL PETERSON & LEONARD ZAICHKOWSKY, PHD

overtime thriller against the Georgia Bulldogs. It was Saban's sixth national championship tying his idol, former Alabama coach Paul "Bear" Bryant, for most all-time in the modern era of the sport.

At the end of the last decade, pundits hailed that game as one of the most exciting and competitive of the last ten years, not only in college football but across all sports. Georgia entered the game as four point underdogs to the perennial powerhouse Alabama, even though Clemson upset Saban's squad a year earlier in the title game. That loss motivated the Crimson Tide from the final whistle to the first day of Spring practice to the opening week of the 2017-18 season where Saban told the SEC media, "Hopefully, we don't waste a failure."[1] His coaching method, popularly known as The Process, takes its origin from his days as a young defensive coordinator with the Cleveland Browns. There he worked for another aspiring coach, Bill Belichick, who was instilling his own succinct but motivational mantra to "do your job." Today, almost thirty years later, they are the most successful head coaches in the history of college and professional football, respectively, with six championship trophies each.

So, when the Bulldogs went into the locker room at halftime with a 13 point lead, having held Alabama to just 21 passing yards, Nick Saban knew he must make a change. Not just a tweak to his playbook, not just an encouraging rant to his players, but a fundamental shift in his game plan. He called together two of his quarterbacks, starter Jalen

Hurts and backup Tua Tagovailoa, to tell them that Tua would start the second half. At that point in his college career, the freshman Tagovailoa had yet to start a game, so inserting him into the national championship at halftime, down by two touchdowns, seemed illogical to fans and commentators. But they cautiously gave Saban, already a legend, the benefit of the doubt.

The decision became one for the ages, as Tua resuscitated Alabama with 166 yards of second half passing and three touchdowns including the game winning 41-yard throw to DeVonta Smith on the second play of their overtime possession. Despite his usual stoic, "take what the opponent gives you" demeanor, Saban is the same coach who called an onside kick with the score tied in the national title game two years earlier against Clemson. That successful conversion and drive ended with a touchdown leading to his fifth trophy.

And while these extraordinary decisions get the headlines, Saban would be the first to remind us of the hundreds of micro-decisions made by his players, the opponents and the officials throughout any four quarters. Even in that 2018 game, fast, in-the-moment decisions, both good and bad, contributed to the outcome. Decisions to pass to a certain receiver, to use a different technique against a lineman, to overreact and retaliate against an opponent, or to throw a momentum shifting penalty flag change the moment, which, taken together, change the outcome.

Nothing happens in a game without a decision, whether

it be a conscious choice or a subconscious reaction to an ever-changing set of stimuli. Post game analyses lament the mental mistakes and the missed opportunities. Just as often, the clutch plays and the appearance of genius insight garner praise. However, consistent, superior decision-making is part of "your job" as an athlete, coach or official.

Inside the play-by-play minutiae of sport, each choice stands on its own as a drop of water that still contributes to the full glass. And that is all one person can focus on at any one time, just his or her next action in the next play. Blocking everything else out is the only way to manage the noise from a thousand variables that only confuse the brain. Those tiny, consecutive steps create the process that Saban preaches. Think of this compartmentalization as being present in the moment. "Don't think about winning the SEC Championship," said Saban. "Don't think about the national championship. Think about what you needed to do in this drill, on this play, in this moment. That's the process: Let's think about what we can do today, the task at hand."[2]

In our 2018 book, <u>"The Playmaker's Advantage"</u>,[3] we explored the mind of a player like Tagovailoa - one that can take over a game with superior "athlete cognition." Actually, we coined that term trying to describe the mental process that repeated itself hundreds of times a game. Athlete cognition consists of three interwoven sub-processes; Search-Decide-Execute or See-Think-Do. The first and last parts build on decades of research on perception and skill acquisition, respectively. But the mushy middle is still a mystery. What goes on inside the "black box" of decision-making hides from view. We can prepare an athlete with pre-game information and tactics, then recap their decision quality post-game. But getting under the hood to work on the engine of decisions is more difficult.

Buying a new car or evaluating a loan application or planning a vacation are processes that combine the input of data, a decision algorithm, and the output of a plan. And while the consequences of those types of decisions may be significant, there is a unique approach to arriving at the best option. In those scenarios, there is time to collect more information, as well as hours if not days to process, ponder and predict possible outcomes. However, in a game, competition, or any high pressure environment, the crucible of tension dictates a faster process.

In sports, just as in any action-oriented activity, vision and perception provide the input while our well-trained motor skills deliver the output. Go left or go right? Pass or shoot? Foul or don't foul? Given the same sensory details from a chaotic game environment, how and why do players make different choices? In post-game reviews, they regret the errors, sometimes surprised that they were capable of such a blunder. Just as confusing is the unconscious flow that can place them squarely in the zone where decisions come instantly and effortlessly, leading to an outstanding performance.

And that's why we continued the search, this time drilling down into the muddy middle. After reading our first book, coaches and players asked us to pull back the curtain to see who is controlling the levers, specifically on what drives decisions and how to train this skill.

The Athlete Decision Model

As with the Athlete Cognition process, Dr. Len and I knew we needed to visualize a new framework to talk about the decision-making process. We have cleverly named this the Athlete Decision Model or ADM (see Figure 1). We tried hard to brainstorm a catchy acronym but opted for simplicity. Given the input of their surroundings through sight, sound, and a mental radar of those around them, players may perceive varying degrees of reality. So, the raw material that they have to work with to make their next decision is not equal. In the same way, the only tangible outcome of a decision is the action taken by the player. We know that a running back decided to cut left then right because we see it live. The skill requires and follows the decision. But how well he executes that move, the quickness and the angle of direction change, is a motor skill that combines some genetic gifts but mostly with what we call hours of deliberate, intentional practice. Plenty of running backs may choose the same elusive maneuver but may not have the same jaw-dropping control of gravity that a playmaker possesses. These are abilities on both the front end and back end of a decision that vary from player to player, and determine which decisions are possible and their final execution.

Figure 1: Athlete Decision Model™

Part 1 - Traits - Knowing Who We Are

Traits define who we are at a moment in time. Some traits are locked for life, some are moldable. Athletes can improve both their vision and perception with the help of advanced vision screening and occulomotor exercises. Eye-tracking technology captures and measures their anticipation of an opponent's next move. And players of all ages know all too well about drills to improve their technical skills in their sport. Constant practice of passing, shooting and defending builds the underlying skill database for use in a game. But exactly how our brain uses the current snapshot of perception and skill to make hundreds of decisions in a game is what we have focused on in this book.

Along with a player's ability to take in their surroundings and execute the chosen skill, there are three other important traits that are uniquely their own; attention, cognition and emotion. Attention is not just perception, taking in the outside world through our senses, but rather what our brain priortizes as relevant to our immediate needs, excluding surrounding stimuli. For a variety of reasons that we'll discuss, we are drawn to a certain focus intentionally or subconsciously which can be good or bad. In sports, hours of play design and practice are devoted to fooling the opponent with different "looks" or formations, false signals intended to draw our attention away from the real threat. Even specific skill moves like the crossover in basketball or the stepover in soccer have a single purpose, to distract an opponent's attention. The playmakers have learned ways to maintain their focus and not be fooled.

We define cognition as the speed and capacity of a player's brain to decide. It is the athlete's personal neuroscience, mixing their working memory capacity with their brain's information processing speed. This is not intelligence, per se, but the raw horsepower of the cognitive machinery in our heads. As our research review will show, some of this brain power is inherited but can still improve. The vast archive of neuroplasticity studies show that we do not have a static, slow brain. Just as with 40-yard dash times and bench press bests, we can build our neuro fitness with the right tools and activities. We can measure and maximize our simple reaction time, choice reaction time, problem solving, and memory efficiency for a player's specific sport.

Then there is the trait that defines sport more than any other - emotion. At the highest levels, thousands of screaming fans pack stadiums while millions watch at home. But even at the local level, family, friends and neighbors cheer on their sons and daughters. Tonight's star performance becomes tomorrow's headlines in the town newspaper. Walking the high school hallways after a big win is the reward that drives players to excel in the game. But with the adulation comes enormous pressure. Self-confidence can rise and fall like a roller coaster during a game, during a half or even minute by minute. Fear of failure directly affects decision-making, as does the will to win. Coaches can pretend that their players should make logical decisions during a game, but for those that have played, they know that's not always possible.

Understanding and embracing emotions helps players factor their presence into their decision-making process. Intertwined with their feelings is the overriding effect of fatigue. As it saps energy levels, decision quality sinks with them. Both erode working memory and processing speed as the game wears on and the stakes increase. Much of traditional sport psychology deals with training techniques to manage emotions, both pre-game and in-game. Making fast, intuitive decisions requires rising above the filters of feelings and fatigue. Part 2 of this book deals exclusively with these three traits, attention, cognition and emotion.

Part 2 - Constraints - Knowing The Boundaries

While traits reflect who we are, and to a degree, who we can become, there are other forces at work on our sport decisions. These constraints are out of our direct control, yet they put boundaries on creativity within the game. And by creativity, we mean the freedom to play the game however we want.

The first and most obvious constraint are the sport's set of rules. Without them, any game would be pure chaos. As athletes, rules are the first lessons we learn. Taking over two steps without dribbling the basketball is against the rules. Crossing the line of scrimmage before the snap of the football is offsides. Passing a soccer ball to a teammate who has already run past the last defender is also offsides, but with a different definition. Hockey and football are contact sports, but only to a certain degree before rules get broken.

The arbiter of rules is the referee or umpire, someone whose sole responsibility is to ensure a fair competition. But why is there a need for an official with a whistle to stop the play and enforce rules? Shouldn't both teams simply follow the rules in the spirit of good sportsmanship? Obviously, we know the answer; players are humans and humans are prone to cheat, all in the name of victory and those emotional highs. Quite a few of the rule infractions called in a game seem on purpose. Everything from common faults like a lineman hanging on a little too long to a defender to prevent a tackle to a World Series winning baseball team creating an elaborate system to warn their batters of the pitch type up next.

In this book, we will focus only on the spontaneous, momentary, but rule-breaking actions rather than the premeditated, organized cheating that is a topic for future sport psychology/ethics studies.

Those "on-purpose" infractions imply a conscious decision to break the rules. They may be unplanned seconds before the incident, but they happened because of an instant decision. The cornerback thought he had the wide receiver covered until he didn't and needed to break up the pass even if he knew he caused pass interference. But then there are the calls for mistakes that resulted, most likely, from lack of focus rather than ill intent.

In fact, for the last three NFL seasons, four of the top ten most called penalties were for false start, defensive offside, neutral zone infraction and delay of game.[4] These professional players, the best in the world, still make these errors at least once or twice per game. They know they shouldn't and they hear about it from their coaches, teammates and fans. Yet, it still happens. In our chapter on Rules, we dig deeper into how the brain stores, manages and recalls the rules framework. Whether its intentional attempts to cheat or lapses in focus and attention, knowing how to teach and train players to minimize fouls, penalties and turnovers is an obvious but often overlooked mission.

While rules are universal to all players and teams in a sport, tactics are the domain of the coach. Especially in team sports, but also important in individual sports, having an overall strategy followed by specific tactics against an opponent is the only way to make sure that coach and player are on the same page. Nick Saban defaulted to a quarterback starter who had led the team throughout the season, through the semi-final game and into the championship. The tactics and, therefore, the playbook assumed Jalen Hurts was running the offense. Even though Alabama had a plan, it stopped working (the Crimson Tide got "hit in the mouth" as Mike Tyson likes to say). The moment required a major tactic change and the players, especially on offense, needed to adapt.

Just like rules establish a set of constraints in the brain, a coach's instructions require programming and recall during a heated game. For younger players, it is a matrix of if-then rules that, hopefully, simplify the options so creative thinking is unnecessary when a defender is bearing down. But the spectrum of tactical directions runs a wide gamut of tightly controlled actions to a looser style of play. Each coach, depending on their level of faith in their players, creates an environment of either control or experimentation. The consequence of not following a coach's tactical plan is to be yelled at from the sideline or even substituted out of the game.

So, along with the mind blurring pace of play, the inexperienced midfielder needs to monitor his decisions so they match with what he was told repeatedly in practice and summarized before kickoff. Was I supposed to attack the left side of the defense? Or was that in Tuesday's game? What was the tendency of this attacker coming at me? My teammate is open in the middle, but that means I have to pass it across the field. The last time I did that, the coach yelled at me.

How does the brain overlay a tactical plan and all the "best practice" reminders that come with learning a sport? How are these bits of information accessed within a second when needed? As with technical skills, there needs to be an automaticity of decision-making. Don't think, react. But how is that taught? We will look at the latest decision research and how top coaches instill their game plans into their players.

And then there is time, the most pressing constraint to any fast-paced sport. If given enough time, athletes would make more consistent and correct decisions, uncovering and testing options that may lay hidden. They consider what-if scenarios, apply the test data and compare the solutions to yield an optimized winner. But across sports, the clock is an equal opponent. Whether its four quarters, three periods, or two halves, the boundaries of time add pressure to the situation.

Then there are additional time constraint rules within the game. The NFL's 40-second play clock has caused the delay of game penalty to be among the top ten most called. The NBA is littered with time limits: the 24-second shot clock, the 8-second rule for crossing mid-court, the 5-second rules for in-bounding and closely guarded man, and the 3-

second lane violation. The NHL has 2, 4, 5 or 10-minute penalties. In soccer, the referee can add extra time to the end of the game and, coming in 2022, MLB is planning to roll out the 20-second pitch clock. Most speed up the game or penalize one team for a foul, but have also inserted a sense of urgency to not only beat your opponent but the clock. These in-game clocks act like other rules, layering on another set of constraints for players to monitor. But at least a fixed number of seconds define these rules.

By far, a player's timing is disrupted the most by the unpredictable pressure from an opponent. A winger in hockey receives a cross-ice pass, knowing that he has less than two seconds to control the puck, scan the opportunities, decide on an action and make his move before a defender is checking him into the boards. A quarterback is taught to keep an internal clock ticking in his head after the snap, knowing that, in less than three seconds, he must release the ball or run before the oncoming blitz puts him on the ground. When his offensive line does their job, commentators love the phrase, "he's got all day back there" which in reality means up to six seconds. An inexperienced junior player who has stepped up to the next level waits for that golden moment when "the game slows down for him."

Consistently making quick, accurate decisions is the unique advantage of playmakers. Other players can, perhaps, match her physical speed, strength and size. But maintaining her attention and processing information quickly while managing her emotions under the constraints of time, rules and tactics differentiates the playmaker from her peers.

Throughout the first two-thirds of the book, we will explain these concepts in more detail, while telling stories of how playmakers across many sports rise to the occasion. Talking about it is helpful, but players and coaches also want ideas on how to implement training programs that emphasize better decision-making. We have left Part 3 for just that purpose.

Part 3 - Pursuit of the Perfect Decision

One question that kept coming up when we were planning this book was "What is the perfect decision?" There is some agreement among those in sports on what the perfect decision is not; penalties, turnovers, allowing a scoring play or failing to score ourselves. When we create a turnover in our favor or complete a pass or capitalize on a scoring opportunity, we hail the decisions of players. But because the decision made in the muddy middle of a player's brain is only demonstrated by a successful series of actions, we cannot be sure if it was the decision or the execution or possibly a better decision by the opponent that prevented a successful outcome. Think of the hundreds of passes made in any basketball, hockey or soccer game at any level. Can we identify and rate each one in terms of quality, using either a binary metric of right/wrong or a sliding scale of, say, 1 to 10?

The problem is that we don't know what didn't happen. A defenseman passed the puck to his right winger, but the play broke down with a turnover. Later in the same shift, the same defenseman made the same pass to the same teammate, who then eluded a defender and scored a goal. In the stats, the defenseman was two for two in completed passes with an assist for the goal. The second pass, even though it was the same as the first, appears to be the right or "perfect" pass because the outcome of the play was a goal.

But what should we rate the first pass decision? Was there a different opportunity to pass to another teammate? Did we miss a scoring opportunity because of a sub-optimal initial pass? Maybe that first pass could have been a half second earlier or to his teammate's right side instead of his left. But we'll never know. All we can consider is what happened. During film review, we can suggest a different pass in that situation, but the chances of that exact sequence of player positioning, timing and angles may never happen again.

Which brings us back to the training problem. Every coach and player we have talked with wants to improve their decision-making. But improvement implies moving from point A to point B, from lesser quality to higher quality. All the collected data inundates coaches and players, which is fuel for analysts to find patterns by asking better questions.

Statistics, however, helps test those questions, within a hypothesis, to improve the quality of our answers. Coaches and players need both to measure not only individual decisions but also to find opportunities to exploit a specific opponent or a pattern that has succeeded over many opponents.

So, we look at improvement from the perspective of the individual player and the team. We explore the world of sports analytics to uncover advanced methods of data manipulation using manual and machine learning techniques. Then, we overlay those stats on to the weave of traits and constraints to suggest best practices that players and coaches can work on together.

Because the game comes down to individual players doing their individual jobs through every decision. Each person has to perform within the constraints given while maximizing their own cognitive traits to deliver for their team. As Coach Belichick said about his players way back in 2000: "The main point to me is that they have to be coordinated and the 10 people have to support what that 11th guy is doing, and vice versa.... The only way that can happen is for there to be discipline, for everyone to be disciplined enough to do their job, knowing the guy beside him is doing his, too, so that you can count on him and he can count on you, and go right down the line."[5]

PART I

TRAITS

1

ATTENTION

"Attention is what steers your perceptions; it's what controls your reality. It's the gateway to the mind."

— Apollo Robbins

For a man who takes no joy in facing the media, mumbling his way through most of his answers, Bill Belichick will light up the room when he sees greatness. Sitting at a table with Cris Collinsworth, Deion Sanders and NFL Network host Rich Eisen, Belichick welcomed former Baltimore Ravens safety Ed Reed into the NFL's list of 100 greatest players.

"You're the best free safety that has ever played this

game that I've seen," Belichick said with an uncharacteristic enthusiasm. "You're awesome."[1]

As Collinsworth told a story of Reed intercepting fellow Hall of Famer Peyton Manning, Belichick couldn't contain himself, jumping in before Collinsworth had set the scene.

"I'm sure he was dreaming about it at night," said Belichick with a bit of giddiness pointing at Reed. "He opens in the middle of the field. As soon as he takes two steps to the midfield, he turns his back on the quarterback and beats [wide receiver Reggie] Wayne to the ball. Best play I've ever seen a free safety make."

To add some clarification on the snap of the ball, Reed pretended to break to the middle of the field, knowing that Manning would check his position and direction before he threw the ball. But Reed had devoured game film of the Colts quarterback during the week and found a rare cue that he could exploit.

"Peyton, on that particular play, studying him that week, if he pumps that way, he throws that way. So, if you look at the play, you'll see Peyton actually pump that way first and when he looked back, he looked at me. And I look like I'm going to the middle. So, as I'm studying him that week, I'm like, this is a gimmie."

"You knew that Peyton knew what you would do," said Collinsworth. "And so you did the opposite of what he had been studying. He made a career out of thinking what you're thinking and doing the opposite. And he said it was the first time someone thought what he was thinking and got him back again."

As he walked to the sideline after that play, Manning stared down the field with a confused look and a subtle shake of his head, an unusual sight for one of the game's best. But he wasn't surprised. In the week leading up to that game, a reporter asked Manning about Reed, who the reporter described as "one of the best safeties in the league." Manning caught the error quickly, "I was going to correct you. He is the best safety in the league, and has been really for this past decade."[2]

As a teammate for a short time, Sanders added his praise by making a case that Reed, inducted into the Hall of Fame as a safety, could have been a great cornerback. "He had the skill set, the anticipation, the speed… everything it took to be a corner."[3]

Anticipation and speed, a fundamental pairing of cognitive and physical skills that playmakers possess. Anticipation built on preparedness, visual search behavior, and pattern recognition with the counter-balancing art of disguise and deception. And speed, not just of feet, but of the brain's information processing rate that can make decisions faster than an opponent.

In our previous book, The Playmaker's Advantage, we touched on the role of visual perception, or the "search" phase of the Athlete Cognition Cycle. For a more detailed look at vision skills, we encourage you to explore that section of the book. Since our focus here is on the decision-making process, we want to dive into the cognitive processing that precedes a decision during a game. Taking in the world through our senses is a study of its own, but what a player does with that information as fuel for the hundreds if not thousands of choices he needs to make is the crux of our journey.

The Cat and Mouse Game

In 1996, when Eddie Perez arrived for Spring Training with the Atlanta Braves, he assumed he would continue his role of backup catcher to Javy Lopez. But with the departure of Charlie O'Brien, a role became available that was impossible to pass up - to be the primary catcher for Hall of Fame pitcher, Greg Maddux. The four-time Cy Young award winner preferred to develop a deep relationship with one catcher and with Lopez busy with the other aces of the Braves staff, Tom Glavine and John Smoltz, Maddux put his faith in the second-year, Venezuelan-born catcher. The battery lasted for five seasons and 121 of the 744 games pitched by Maddux, forty more games than any other pairing.

At first, it was a master-student relationship as Maddux, still to this day considered one of the best pitchers in MLB history, taught Perez his extraordinarily detailed analysis of every hitter in the National League. After taking the assignment, Perez recalled succinct advice given to him from the other Braves catchers and their manager, "They just said, 'This guy is smart, whatever he wants to do, let him do it.'[4] "

In their third season together, the balance of knowledge was evening out with Perez feeling more like an equal partner. He recalled one game in mid-August against the Houston Astros. The Braves were comfortably ahead, 4-0 late in the game. Maddux had always instructed Perez that they would never pitch inside to Astros' slugger Jeff Bagwell, to avoid his sweet spot. But in this game, with Bagwell at the plate, Maddux went off-script and threw an inside fastball which Bagwell launched over 500 feet foul. Undeterred, and to Perez's surprise, Maddux again offered a tempting pitch right in Bagwell's inside wheelhouse, which the All-Star seized on, sending it into the left field bleachers.

The Braves prevailed, but Perez felt cheated and said so to his pitcher. "I was mad," he said. "After the game, I was like, 'Why? We could have struck him out like we always do.' But he was like, 'They have a good team and they might be in the playoffs a few months from now.' But I was like, 'Whatever, dude, I want the complete game and I'm not worried about three months from now.'[5] "

Sure enough, in the Fall during game 1 of the National League Division Series between the Braves and the Astros, Maddux threw a perfect first inning, striking out Bagwell with a selection of pitches, all away on the outside corners. Perez remembered what Maddux told him.

"When we were walking back to the dugout, he said, 'Do you remember two months ago?' I had already forgot about it. But he said [Bagwell] was looking for the [inside] pitch the whole time. Then he turned around and laughed. That's something I'm never going to forget."[6]

Just as Ed Reed had studied Peyton Manning to unearth a subtle nugget of vulnerability, Maddux had set-up Bagwell by giving him a moment of glory in a meaningless inning only to use it against him in a crucial playoff game. But Bagwell is not alone. Maddux flummoxed plenty of other All-Star hitters.

"It seems like he's inside your mind with you," said Hall of Famer Wade Boggs. "When he knows you're not going to swing, he throws a straight one. He sees into the future. It's like he has a crystal ball hidden inside his glove."[7]

"The mental side of this game is vital, and it carries over into your physical execution," said longtime Braves pitching coach, Leo Mazzone. "He relishes it. He gets a great thrill out of outfoxing somebody or setting them up for the kill."

Speaking of Glavine, who won the NL Cy Young award the year before Maddux's record four consecutive wins, he praised his teammate and friend. "I think he's got a gift. He's able to notice things in the course of a game that no one else can—the way a hitter may open up a little, move up in the box an inch, change his stance. I've tried to be aware of that stuff. I really have. But I'm so focused on what I'm trying to do. I don't know how he does it."[8]

Just like the proverbial chain, a team is only as good as

its individual players and their second by second decisions. Learning to make the best choice at the moment does not happen in a vacuum. The process is a constant cat-and-mouse game between the player and her opponent as each tries to not only proactively "do the right thing" but is also plotting to disrupt, disguise and deceive the available options for the other. This happens at a micro-level of visual illusions, like physical dekes and feints, and also at a macro-level of cognitive illusions, such as the unexpected pitch or play call.

Smoke and Mirrors

In another entertainment arena, these illusions create what is better known as magic. Sleight-of-hand, "now you see it-now you don't" tricks that leave the viewer with that same look that Manning had coming off the field; "How'd he do that?" They play with our focus and our attention, manipulating our visual cortex into expecting the pattern we've seen before but pulling the rug out from under us at the last second.

Hitters often compared Maddux to a magician. Back in 2008, Sports Illustrated writer Joe Posnanski described his favorite pitcher this way. "That was Maddux, always trying something new, always finding an edge, always formulating a plan. He showed you the quarter, made the quarter disappear, pulled the quarter out of your ear only now it was a half dollar, and it was blue, made that disappear, turned it into a Buick, it was all an old-fashioned magic show and come to think of it that might be why I liked Maddux so much."[9]

A dozen years later, Posnanski was still reveling in the trickery of Maddux and the dazed hitters of the day who couldn't quite figure him out.

"It was more like they had the reaction people have when they see a particularly awe-inspiring magic trick," wrote Posnanski in The Athletic. "You will see people wandering out of a David Copperfield show in Las Vegas, and they are a little bit dazed, a little bit confused, a little bit angry at themselves that they couldn't quite figure out how that car appeared or how he knew the exact numbers that people in the audience would choose."

To reinforce the magician analogy, Posnanski went a step further. "The magician Teller offered one of my favorite magic quotes to Esquire's Chris Jones when he said: 'Sometimes magic is just spending more time on something than anyone else might reasonably expect.' Maddux's magic, at least part of it, came from thinking about pitching at such depths that it went beyond what even hitters might reasonably expect."[10]

He has a good point. Magic is, of course, not magic but well-rehearsed distractions. In fact, neuroscience and magic have a lot in common. As Teller, widely known as one half of the famed Penn and Teller show, quipped, "Magicians have done controlled testing in human perception for thousands of years."[11] And two neuroscientists, Drs. Stephen Macknik and Susana Martinez-Conde of the Barrow Neurological Institute, took note and started a research agenda to understand the connection. They partnered with an honor roll of Vegas magicians and illusionists, including Teller, Mac King, Johnny Thompson (The Great Tomsoni), James Randi and celebrity pickpocket Apollo Robbins to map the art of deception and attention diversion to their underlying cognitive constructs.[12]

"Neuroscientists are just beginning to catch up with the magician's facility in manipulating attention and cognition," wrote Macknik and Martinez-Conde in a Scientific American article summarizing their research. "Of course the aims of neuroscience are different from those of magic; the neuroscientist seeks to understand the brain and neuron underpinnings of cognitive functions, whereas the magician wants mainly to exploit cognitive weaknesses. Yet the techniques developed by magicians over centuries of stage magic could also be subtle and powerful probes in the hands of neuroscientists, supplementing and perhaps expanding the instruments already in experimental use."[13]

Just as in the Reed vs Manning and the Maddux vs Bagwell showdowns, magicians master misdirection of attention. They use terms like the "effect," the coin produced from the ear of a spectator, and the "method," the secret of how they palmed the coin in their hand when reaching towards the ear. Hiding the method well produces the illusion of an effect that seems unexplainable. This distraction can be overt, grabbing the spectator's gaze and attention with a gesture or noise away from the method, or covert, by stealing attention away despite a direct focus on the method. For example, while a spectator is staring at a sleight of hand trick, intent on finding the ruse, the magician uses covert misdirection by distracting attention with a joke or a movement that seems natural.

In fact, Macknik and Martinez-Conde worked again with pickpocket master Robbins on research showing a specific movement could better fool spectators. In the well-known coin vanishing trick, Robbins holds a coin in his left forefinger and thumb, covers it with his right hand, then moves the right fist away from the empty left fingers. When he opens his right hand with no coin (the effect), the spectator's eyes and brain immediately searched for an explanation.

Through years of demonstrating the trick, Robbins had learned that a curvilinear motion of his right hand held the spectator's gaze longer after the big reveal than a straight-lined motion. Sure enough, Macknik and Martinez-Conde tested several volunteers with eye-tracking glasses and proved Robbins correct. From this simple experiment built on years of practice, the researchers saw enormous potential insight.

"These findings may have far-reaching implications beyond magic, such as in the application of predator-evasion strategies in the natural world, in military tactics, in sports misdirection, and in marketing. This research also demonstrates that magic theory can provide new windows into the psychological and neural principles of perception and cognition."[14]

Harvard researchers Daniel Simons and Christopher Chabris created the best-known covert misdirection demonstration with their "focus on the basketball passes" experiment. While diligently counting the number of passes, as instructed by the research team, study volunteers, along with millions of us since then, completely miss the appearance of a dancing gorilla crossing the screen. Our focus was intense, but our attention was distracted, a phenomenon labeled "sustained in-attentional blindness."[15] If you have not watched the video,[16] give it a try, even though we just gave away the punchline.

Macknik and Martinez-Conde distinguish this "blindness" as a cognitive illusion, different from an optical illusion in that higher-level cognitive functions are fooled rather than our senses. As they explain, "Visual illusions occur because neural circuits in the brain amplify, suppress, converge and diverge visual information in a fashion that ultimately leaves the observer with a subjective perception that is different from the reality."[17]

In the same way that we can separate attention and focus, so can the brain's assumption of motion. The ball and cup routine is a favorite of Penn and Teller. It has evolved from solid, red plastic cups and a wadded up ball of tinfoil to transparent cups and balls of varying sizes, including a baseball. In a whirl of hand movements, balls seem to appear and disappear from where Teller placed them. And small balls become larger balls, then one changes completely to a baseball. So convincing and confusing, the act was the subject of another Macknik and Martinez-Conde paper.[18]

But then when two of the greatest sleight-of-hand performers host their own TV show to invite other artists to fool them, then the deception has reached a new level. On Penn & Teller syndicated show, "Fool Us", that's exactly what Doc Dixon, a comic magician, did with his version of the traditional shell game where he hides a pea under one shell, move them around, then asks the audience to guess its location. But for this episode, Dixon added some puzzling quirks to the routine, which Penn and Teller failed to figure out, gaining him their coveted "Fooled Us" trophy.[19]

"Action is motion with a purpose," says Teller.[20] Thanks to our mirror neurons, that fire whether we're performing an action or observing someone else, our brain understands the logical outcome of a motion. If you make a throwing motion, someone watching will assume you have projected an object. If you move to your right, an observer's brain will assume you will continue to move to your right. This neurological process of priming gives the viewer a preview of what is going to happen next.

"Priming is a type of repetition effect in which the presentation of a stimulus that is similar to a target makes subsequent presentations of the target perceptually more salient," write Macknik and Martinez-Conde. "Priming is used experimentally, and by the magician, to affect the subject's sensitivity to a later presentation of a particular stimulus. Moreover, repetition can be used to induce sensory illusions. Magicians also use repetition to hide the method behind the trick: when observers see an effect repeated, they naturally assume that each repetition is done by the same method."[21]

Back to sports, two obvious magical moves come to mind that imitate the fast hands of Teller or the shell movement of Dixon, basketball's crossover dribble and soccer's step over feints. As a defender against either, the effect is to decide which direction the attacker is going to move past you. Again, our mirror neurons observe a movement one way and assume that objects in motion tend to stay in motion, thanks to Sir Isaac Newton and eight-grade physics class. Wanting to avoid the embarrassment of being fooled by an opponent, we want to decide immediately on the best defense to stop the ball. But as in a magician's priming, that is exactly the folly that they are hoping for. Let's look at each of these moves and decipher their effectiveness.

The Ankle Breakers

Despite being around for over 100 years, the step over, when executed properly, still befuddles defenders, either sending them tumbling over their own feet or standing still as the attacker darts by them. Pedro Calomino, the legendary right winger for Boca Juniors in Argentina, is credited with inventing the move. It migrated to Europe in the 1920s and 30s, becoming soccer's version of sleight-of-hand. The aim is to freeze the defender in a second of indecision or force him into a rash decision to stick out a leg, hoping to separate the ball from the attacker. Forward speed is the secret of the move as the defender must backpedal while maintaining eyes on the ball. Ironically, the ball often travels in a straight line towards the defender while the attacker jab steps one way only to plant his foot in the ground and dart back the other direction.

Originally, the step over was just that, one sharp step to get the defender's center of gravity shifted than a cut back with a tap of the ball. The Brazilians added flair to the move with mesmerizing double and triple step overs. Denilson in the 60s, Ronaldo in the 90s and Ronaldhino in the early 2000s all added individuality and flair to the deceptive move. Portugal's Cristiano Ronaldo made it his signature move, so much so that in his early days at Manchester United, he heard about it from his manager, Sir Alex Ferguson. "Of course, in the beginning of my career he was so important to me because I moved from Sporting to Manchester and had that Portuguese mentality–too many stepovers, decision-making was not the best," said Ronaldo.[22]

Watching hundreds of step over video highlights by

these talented players reveals a few common threads, even among their stylistic differences. The defender is often focused on the ball rolling towards them, but their peripheral vision tracks the exaggerated foot movement as it slices out to one side. Convinced that the attacker has made their decision and picked a side, they often lunge in with a tackle transferring all of their weight onto that front foot. The attacker then "steps over" the ball and the defender's outstretched leg, taking off in the opposite direction often at full speed. Those first few "true" steps away from the defender are at a higher acceleration, leaving behind the flatfooted defender.

This art of deception seems to have considerable science behind it. Several research teams have singled out the step over in soccer or the side step in rugby to understand human perception and how to fool it. In 2018, UK and Australian researchers used occlusion methods to not only show that experienced soccer players are fooled less often than novice players, (a rather common sense hypothesis), but also pulled back the curtain on where they focused their attention before deciding.

Across several earlier studies, they have shown the superiority of experienced playmakers over developing players in judging between a genuine versus a deceptive move across rugby, soccer, football, volleyball and basketball.[23] But the key question is not that they're better, but why? What exactly are the playmakers focused on that the developing players are missing?

For sports like soccer or hockey where the ball or puck are at their feet, or basketball where the ball is dribbled below the waist, should the focus be on the ball or on the lower body? Or is the center of mass, the hips for example, the best place to track as coaches and some pop stars say, "the hips don't lie." Perhaps it is the entire package, upper body, lower body and some sense of a "global processing" that an experienced defender performs when facing a 1v1 situation.

In the 2018 study, Robin Jackson and Bruce Abernethy and their team recruited 48 female soccer players, half considered expert and half who were developing. They asked the players to watch dozens of video clips of an attacking player dribbling towards them and then say out loud if the attacker would go to their left or right. The researchers manipulated the video clips with both spatial and temporal occlusion. For spatial occlusion, they showed clips of the entire attacker's body, then blocked out the upper half, then the lower half of the body. This was to isolate the kinematic information available to the 48 test volunteers. In addition, they also occluded (blocked) the video at four different time stops; 240 ms before the attacker touched or stepped over the ball, 120 ms, 0 ms and 120 ms after. By stopping the videos before the actual move took place, the viewers' decisions keyed on any clues available on which direction the attacker would go.

Occlusion tests are very useful tools in athlete perception research, with applications in baseball pitch recognition, tennis and volleyball serves, penalty kick direction, etc. While a player cannot always verbalize how they knew what would happen next, they can learn to pick up cues that contribute to their subconscious decision-making. Whether used for assessments or training, occluding parts of the visual scene and the time available can sharpen the specific skill set.

Jackson, Abernethy, et al. confirmed that experienced playmakers can better distinguish which direction an attacker will go across both spatial and time occlusions. But they also found that while the lower body or full body images helped their accuracy, they still held an advantage over novice players across all three spatial occlusions. With half of all the video clips, including a deceptive move (a stepover in this case), they outperformed the inexperienced players by picking up bodily cues up to a third of a second before they executed the move. Some telltale sign gave away the attacker's intent.

But what exactly is going on inside the brains of these athletes? While it seems logical that more experienced players are better at anticipating a deceptive movement, our job is to explain why. A 2013 study[24] by Dr. Daniel Bishop and his team at Brunel University, along with the expertise of Dr. Abernethy, designed a very similar experiment, albeit with one technological twist. They asked thirty-nine participants, divided into three levels of soccer skill, to lie in a fMRI (functional magnetic resonance imaging) scanner while viewing video clips of oncoming attackers. So, just at with the Jackson study, the volunteer's job was to predict which direction the video attacker would go with the video being occluded at different times before the actual move took place.

Dr. Bishop's experiment design sought to watch the brain activity of the volunteers while they make that decision. One of his theories was that the mirror neuron system helped more expert players predict the actions of an opponent. The logic goes like this. In the human brain, there are networks of neurons that respond when a person is performing an action, like dribbling a ball towards an opponent. When the attacker decides to cut left or right, or fake left or right, certain regions of the brain can be seen, with fMRI scans, to "light up" with electrical activity.

Back in the 1990s, almost by chance, researchers at the University of Parma found that these same regions were also activated ("mirrored") when we simply watch someone doing the same task. The research started with macaque monkeys eating, then watching others eat, but the studies have now confirmed the same neural behavior in many human activities.

In the same way, Dr. Bishop et al. predicted that expert soccer players use the mirror neuron system to guess the intentions of an attacker. Since they can do these deceptive moves themselves, their brain can also read the mind, if you will, of a player with similar skill. The less-experienced player does not have that move in their tool bag, and therefore cannot see it in others.

As hypothesized by the research team, there were significant differences in prediction skill between the top performers and the intermediate group, and between the intermediate group and the beginners, as measured by the accuracy of their guesses. But now, with their brains being scanned in real-time, the telltale areas of the brain also showed greater activation of mirror neurons for the highest performers compared to the intermediate/beginner groups.

Interestingly, there was little mirror neuron difference between the lower two groups. Perhaps this is a clue as to the playmaker's advantage over average or novice players. As the researchers concluded, "The brain activation differences witnessed may correspond to not only the surpassing of a threshold for hours accumulated in practice/competition to become sufficiently expert, but also the quality of such practice."[25]

This linkage of perception and action is at the core of sport skill training. We often learn how to do something by watching others do it first, then we imitate the fine motor skills required, often badly the first time. Then, with practice, specifically "deliberate practice" as Dr. Anders Ericsson has proposed, we internalize the steps and motions. Once a playmaker has mastered how to perform a stepover move, her brain can call on its "Action Observation Network", including the mirror neurons, to pick out the subtle cues given by her opponent. The cycle of learning movements from others, practicing and mastering on our own, then predicting other's movements comes full circle.

"Our neuroimaging data clearly shows greater activation of motor and related structures in the brains of expert footballers, compared to novices, when taking part in a football-related anticipation task," said Dr. Bishop. "We believe that this greater level of neural activity is something that can be developed through high quality training, so the next step will be to look at how the brain can be trained over time to anticipate the moves of opponents."[26]

If you were to go watch the many highlight videos online of Ronaldo or Ronaldhino, they show dozens of successful stepovers and "blow-bys" of the confused defender. No one makes videos of all the failed stepover attempts where the defender makes the tackle. But in just watching the positive results, the pattern is obvious. The attacker waits for the defender to commit, either by leaning to one side, switching his feet or stabbing at the ball with a foot. Then he makes the last cut to the opposite side.

As the research has shown, the experienced attacker has been on the other side of the ball. Duped before, they learn how to think like a defender, then use that in their favor. Likewise, there are far fewer video highlights of veteran defenders being crossed up on a stepover or other deceptive tricks. They have learned what not to do and rely on their own mirror neurons to signal tiny clues of how to stop the oncoming player.

A legendary AC Milan defender, Paolo Maldini said, "If I have to make a tackle then I have already made a mistake."[27] While defenders into today's games resort to, much to the crowd's delight, for athletic, sliding lunges, sometimes four or five per game, Maldini averaged less than one tackle per game throughout his career while facing some of the greatest playmakers of the last half century.

Xabi Alonso, the equally impressive defensive midfielder for Liverpool, Real Madrid, and Bayern Munich, agrees that anticipation beats reaction every day. "I don't think tackling is a quality. It is something you have to resort to, not a characteristic of your game," Alonso said. "I can't get into my head that football development would educate tackling as a quality, something to learn, to teach, a characteristic of your play. How can that be a way of seeing the game? I just don't understand football in those terms."[28] This instinct to anticipate an attacker's move then getting into a defensive position that stops it is the ultimate training goal. Not to mention avoiding appearances in someone's stepover highlight video.

Hearing Before Seeing

Tennis legend Martina Navratilova knows that hearing is believing.

"You really depend on hearing the ball being hit, particularly when you are at the net," Navratilova said. "You first hear the ball. Then you react to the speed and spin according to the sound. And when you can't hear it, it really throws you off."[29]

And Andy Murray, former world #1 ranked player and two-time Olympic champion, agrees: "We use our ears when we play; it's not just the eyes," said Murray. "It helps us pick up the speed of the ball, the spin that's on the ball, how hard someone's hitting it. If we played with our ears covered or with headphones on, it would be a big advantage if your opponent wasn't wearing them. It's tricky, you know? You can still do it, but it's harder, for sure."[30]

According to research by the National Institutes of Health, we hear faster than we see with auditory reaction times being 140-160 milliseconds versus 180-200 milliseconds for visual stimuli.[31]

So, imagine life as a rising tennis player who always wore headphones, or in Lee Duck-hee's case, was born deaf. All incoming sensory data about the swing, contact and ball would be visual. No sound of the opponent's racket strings striking the ball. Only the kinematic feel of your own racket hitting the ball back without the accompanying ping to let you know if you found the sweet spot.

Despite his limitation, Duck-hee became a phenom on the competitive South Korean junior tennis circuit, winning ten titles on the ITF Junior Circuit. In 2019, at 21, he became the first deaf player to compete in and win an ATP tournament match beating Henri Laaksonen at the Winston-Salem Open. Now ranked in the mid-200s globally, he plans a continued ascent to be a regular competitor on the professional circuit.

"People who were born deaf or hard of hearing may have a stronger sense of intuition in general, and tend to see subtle clues in a person's face or body language better than people with normal hearing," said Paige Stringer, who played for the University of Washington and founded the Global Foundation for Children with Hearing Loss. "They are more visual, because when one sense is compromised, other senses are heightened to compensate. If my hypothesis is correct, people who are deaf or hard of hearing may have an advantage in tennis because they can pick up visual cues faster and better as to their opponent's plans, and may have better reflexes because they see things sooner."[32]

Christopher Rungkat, a top-100 doubles player, agrees with Stringer. "He always seems to know where I am going to hit the ball," said Rungkat. "I don't think he is guessing, it is more like he is reading my mind. Yes, he is fast, but so are a lot of players. If I had to pick one word to sum up his game, I would say anticipation. How he knows where the ball is going off my racquet so early is most impressive."[33]

"Is it possible to have tunnel vision with a hearing impairment?" asks Brian Ehlers, a deaf, two-time Olympic volleyball player. "Yes, the athlete's mind becomes more focused and analytical and creative, as it finds way to utilize the other senses to better coordinate his actions in unison with the projected contact point, velocity and trajectory of the ball."[34]

While Duck-hee learns to overcome his hearing deficit, it upsets players who have long relied on sound on the court that it is being drowned out by a relatively new obstacle - grunting. While we credit Jimmy Connors with the practice of loud, guttural groans when hitting the ball, it has been the women's side of tennis that has caused the most discussion.

Back in 2009, Navratilova did not mince her words, "It is cheating, pure and simple. It is time for something to be done."[35] Maria Sharapova, known for her shrieks during matches, regularly breaks 100 decibels. "From all that grunting, even my throat hurts. I have done that since I was a young girl and just kind of stayed with me. You are absolutely right, my throat hurts all the time after I play matches."[36]

So that players can hear the audible nuances of shots, the chair umpire hushes the crowd before every point. But then the simultaneous timing of racket contact and grunting masks any advantage available, just like Duck-hee faces with every shot. There are two theories as to the potential side effects; either the sudden burst of noise distracts the opposing player which steals attention away from her focus or, as many players claim, they need that sound of contact to anticipate the speed and spin of the ball, something researchers call multi-sensory integration.

In 2019, a team of sport psychologists from Friedrich Schiller University, Jena, led by Dr. Florian Müller and Professor Rouwen Cañal-Bruland, showed a group of experienced tennis players a variety of video clips of a professional tennis match. They occluded the clips at different time intervals after each shot, while the player was letting out a loud grunt. And the researchers also slightly manipulated the volume of the grunts, unbeknownst to the volunteers. They asked the test volunteers to estimate the ball's trajectory and landing spot.

Results showed that louder grunts corresponded with longer estimated ball trajectories, but their level of error was unaffected, supporting the multi-sensory integration viewpoint. "We assume that players account for the physiological benefits provided by grunting," said Dr. Müller. "This possibly explains why an effect can be observed as a result of the grunting, but the ability to anticipate the ball's trajectory remains unaffected."[37]

Just Watch The Ball

For a defensive lineman in football, the simple advice from his coach has remained unchanged, "Don't jump across the line of scrimmage until the center snaps the ball. Just watch the ball." For some of them, the ball is only three feet from their eyes while they stare at it. Yet, jumping offsides is one of the most common penalties among them. And when experienced, NFL defensive players face Aaron Rodgers, quarterback of the Green Bay Packers, they know their eyes have to overrule their ears. Rodgers "hard count" is a mixture of cadence, volume, and pattern disruption in calling out the signals before a snap. "I'd like it to be a foreign language to them," said Rodgers. "They can't quite make out what I'm saying, and they can't get a bead on it, either."[38]

In the 2019 regular season, Rodgers drew opposing defenses offsides four times, one short of his total of five in 2018. Often, that allows a free play, where Rodgers can throw a deep pass with the comfort of knowing that the ensuing offsides will overrule any interception call. In fact, since 2006, Rodgers has attempted 84 passes after a defensive player has jumped early, allowing him to throw over 2000 "air yards", over 900 yards further than any other NFL quarterback during that time period.[39]

Before they met in the 2020 playoffs, three-time Pro Bowl defensive end Jadeveon Clowney stressed the importance of eyes over ears, "We have to be smart. We are in their house - we know they are going to hard count. We know that is a way that he likes to control the game, with his hard count. Letting the play clock going down. We just have to be smart and watch the ball. If we watch the ball, I think we will be OK."[40] But the Packers won that game at Lambeau, and Rodgers got Clowney on a neutral zone infraction penalty.

Even his own linemen have to be careful. T. J. Lang, the former Packers, Pro-Bowl right guard, admitted the need to focus on the snap count and the ball. "Aaron makes it so believable that you kind of start second-guessing yourself when you're at the line," right guard T. J. Lang said. "You might have a split second where you forget and hear his voice, and you've got to watch the ball being snapped. It's amazing what he can do."[41]

The TAIS Model

The ability to concentrate or to focus attention either visually or through another sense may very well be the most important cognitive skill an athlete has. Human attention is a complex process, but Dr. Bob Nideffer simplified the different components of attention with a measuring tool called "The Attentional and Interpersonal Style Inventory" or TAIS to measure attentional strengths and weaknesses, along with the athlete's ability to cope with distractions.

Perhaps the most simple explanation is to see the four categories below as four different television channels and your remote control can switch from channel to channel depending upon the demands of the situation. Athletes with well-practiced attentional skills can quickly switch from having a broad focus to a narrow focus. Also, they can switch from an internal focus to an external focus of attention.

Broad-External or Channel 1

Awareness or "seeing the big picture" and reading all

available cues. Player with excellent field or court sense, reading a rapidly changing environment. For example, a quarterback in football scanning the defense prior to a play starting. Mistakes may be because of paying attention to irrelevant or deceptive cues. May be vulnerable to being faked out easily.

Narrow-External or Channel 2

Focus or locking into one primary target. For example, a baseball hitter zeroing in on the release point of the pitch to read the pitch type and perhaps location. Important skill for blocking out "external" distractions such as fan behavior, trash talk. Athletes can make mistakes if they become too narrow in their focus and miss important peripheral cues (e.g. The "Gorilla" experiment).

Broad-Internal or Channel 3

An "inner big picture" Strategic analysis/planning and dealing with a lot of information. Attentional style of successful coaches. Mistakes may be because of over-analysis and over thinking.

Narrow-Internal or Channel 4

Focused inner thoughts. Important for body awareness, and situational awareness, and mental imagery. For example, a golfer imagining the speed and direction of a crucial putt. Mistakes result in "choking" behavior. Athlete distracted by internal thoughts and become inflexible.

2

COGNITION

"Mental effort, I would argue, is relatively rare. Most of the time we coast."

— DANIEL KAHNEMAN

He's 6'8", about 250 pounds, built like your grandma's immovable armoire and faster than a few NFL wide receivers. Yet, he plays basketball, ironically labeled a "small forward." And he is constantly swapping places in the public opinion of the top five NBA players of all-time. His "physicality and pace", as the experts like to call size and speed, are his obvious advantages. But the NBA has seen dozens of large, quick bodies who have come nowhere near the success of LeBron James.

What sets him apart from the other 99.5% of professional players is located just behind his eyes and between his ears. Some might call it deep basketball knowledge, others, including James, call it a photographic memory. Regardless of the label, the four-time league MVP displays an uncanny ability to recall specific details about players, tactics, and results from the thousands of games he has played.

"I think it entails understanding time and score, understanding your opponent, understanding your teammates and understanding yourself," said Jason Kidd, an NBA Hall of Famer and now an assistant coach of James' current team, the Los Angeles Lakers. "It's kind of like a movie, but playing at fast forward. I think he plays the game that way in the sense of anticipating what's next. And when you have a high basketball IQ, you understand what's going to happen next before anybody else does."[1]

On display again five days after the 2020 NBA All-Star Game, James recalled the last play of the game, with every pass, move and thought pattern. During the one minute recitation,[2] he gazed straight ahead with an unfocused stare as his memory went to work. The sports media world buzzed for the next two days about James' "photographic memory", but that display was only the tip of the iceberg.

Because, for James, it's not just basketball, which memory researchers would expect - a gifted retention within a chosen domain. His teammates claim he's the same with movies and music, able to cite lines of dialogue and song lyrics at will. He can cite facts from other sports or games he never played in.

"Sometimes when we come into our morning meetings on game days, NBA TV will be on and there will be some classic game on," said former teammate Mario Chalmers. "LeBron will take one look at it and know what game it is. He'll be like, 'Oh, that's Game 2 of the '97 Finals,' before they even put it on the screen."[3]

"Look, we're all professional basketball players, so when LeBron remembers something from a basketball game, even if it's from a few years ago, it doesn't exactly blow me away," said Chris Bosh, another former Heat teammate. "But it's when he remembers other stuff, like stuff he shouldn't even know, where you're like, 'What?!' We'll be watching a football game and he'll be like, 'Yeah, that cornerback was taken in the fourth round of the 2008 draft from Central Florida,' or something. And I'll be like, 'How do you know that?' And he'll be like, 'I can't help it.'"[4]

"It's going to help him play until he's 40," said Kidd. "...His IQ is always going to help him because he's going to be able to take less steps, right? Instead of running a six-mile race, he can run a five-mile race just because of his IQ." Kidd added one more warning. "You're not going to cheat him playing cards. Just know he's paying attention."[5]

This cognitive ability to process recent information while retrieving lessons learned from long-term memory is the mark of a playmaker's decision-making. Attention, perception, working memory and information processing combine to form a core executive function in the brain that is the foundation of making the right choice at the right time.

"If I see the defense is shifting over, and they're bringing two [defenders] to the ball, then I know I have a numbers game on the weak side and it's four-on-three," James told Sports Illustrated. "I've been in those positions so many times throughout my career. I can literally close my eyes and know where my guys are going to be at, and be able to read and react to that."[6]

With playmakers, it is the complete package. There are plenty of sports trivia buffs who can instantly recognize and remember minute details of long ago games. And there are just as many physically gifted athletes who, unfortunately, make the same mental mistake repeatedly.

But being able to load archived patterns of recognition into short-term or working memory while processing the real-time information flood that is pouring in from the senses is the machinery that produces consistently accurate and timely decisions. All the cogs must work together in the brain, or an opportunity will vanish in a split second.

As we discussed in the last chapter, Greg Maddux had an encyclopedic memory of hitter tendencies overall and specifically when facing him. But in the pitch by pitch sequence, Maddux has a moment, maybe 30 seconds, to cycle through the options with his catcher until they agree.

We now know this thinking as "system 2" which requires slower, logical, conscious thought, as opposed to "system 1" thinking that is fast, automatic and reactionary.

In his 2011 book, "Thinking Fast and Slow",[7] Nobel prize-winning psychologist Daniel Kahneman explained how we use both methods to navigate the world, making unconscious decisions without bringing our focused attention to the task (for example, "2+2=?" or how we recognize a face in a crowd or drive mindlessly on a quiet road) versus mental processing that requires concentration (like what is "18*38" or recall the name of the face you just saw or parking your car in a tight space).

Learning a sport is no different. At first, as a young, developing player, we dedicate all of our attention and learning energy to simple tasks like learning to dribble a ball or shoot on target. System 2 is in control while System 1 manages pre-learned tasks like running. During this growth phase, System 1 cannot automatically retrieve the rules and tactics of the game. Constant reminders from hours of playing the sport slowly build the knowledge base that eventually becomes managed by System 1.

The goal is a state of automaticity where System 2 makes only high-level game-defining decisions, much like when James recalls a similar pattern of play from a previous game or film study session at just the right moment to help in the current situation. Just like when Maddux calls the pitch that he knows will cross up this one specific hitter because he's been planning it for months, if not years.

Memory Games

When he's not fooling defensive linemen to jump offsides, Aaron Rodgers is building a catalog of unforgettable plays in his memory, starting with high school, continuing through college and now in his 16th season as the Green Bay Packers quarterback. Like James, Rodgers has awed his teammates and those around the league with a deep recall ability of past moments. For the best playmakers, intense sessions of study help create the neural connections that assist with this Google-like search and retrieve skill.

"There are only a handful of guys that have played the position at that kind of level," said Kurt Warner, a Hall of Fame quarterback. "The great ones have the ability to focus and tune everything else out and see more than the others. Average quarterbacks have tunnel vision. They see what's in front of them. The better you get, the more that tunnel expands and the more guys on the field you see. Guys like Aaron, they see it all in a methodical way, and it's almost as if it happens so slowly that it has time to get etched in their brains."[8]

An intrepid reporter for Sports Illustrated put Rodgers to the test a few years ago, quizzing #12 on a random set of football plays from his career stretching back to high school. Given a short prompt, Rodgers jumped in with vivid detail of the game, the situation, the players involved and the outcome. Here's one sample from a game which was almost 15 years before the interview.

Reporter's background, "A three-star recruit in high school, Rodgers received no FBS scholarship offers, so he went to Butte College, a community college in Northern California, for one year. In a 48-21 Butte victory over Shasta, Rodgers threw six touchdown passes. After taking a moment, he listed all six in the correct order. Local newspaper reports of the game corroborate his account."

Setting: Oct. 12, 2002, Shasta College Memorial Stadium, Redding, California.

Reporter's prompt: "You threw a touchdown pass against Shasta where you rolled out and your knees started to buckle..."

Rodgers: "Oh, yeah. I remember my legs buckling on that one, but I hit Garrett for a touchdown. Shasta was our main rival, and they talked a lot of trash that week in the paper, so we came out and threw six touchdowns against them. I think that one to Garrett was the first one. Then I hit Bobby Bernal. Then I hit Garrett again. Then I hit Bobby on 'Syracuse' and then Garrett again on 'Oregon' which was a backside corner route. Then I hit Leyland Henry, he was No. 6, on a little fly pattern out of the backfield."[9]

These types of players are once in a generation talents, both physically and mentally. And it is not so much the post-game memory feats that players like James and Rodgers display, but the in-game interplay between the fluid environment and the finger-snap decisions that distinguish playmakers. The focus of this chapter is to understand those underlying cognitive components, to uncover clues for identifying and improving young players.

Models of Expertise

Before we launch into the decision-making playbook, let's step back and review some neuropsychology fundamentals. We have mentioned concepts like attention, memory, information processing and executive function but it would be helpful to get a big picture of how these terms interrelate.

When we set out to learn something new, we don't have the procedural knowledge to walk us through the steps needed. It is all new to us, knowing what to pay attention to, try to store that in our memory, try it over and over slowly and then refine the skill until we can do it quickly and automatically. Early on, we rely on our raw cognitive abilities to intake the new information and build a neural model of the activity ready to reuse repeatedly, specifically growing our attentional control, working memory and executive function while increasing our information processing speed.

In the last chapter, we discussed attention along with its cohorts, anticipation and pattern recognition, and its nemesis, deception. Attention requires working memory. In fact, we can define it as the ability to guard items being held in memory by focusing on relevant cues from the environment without being distracted by shiny objects that force working memory to flush its storage in favor of the new stimulus.

A point guard brings the ball up the court with the play that was just called by his coach in the preceding timeout. His working memory keeps the play's action steps ready for his executive function to call on when he pulls the trigger to start the play. But then his opponent pressures him before he gets across mid-court. Now his attention turns towards guarding the ball, getting across center court in time and maintaining his dribble.

His working memory is now being challenged to remember the play and the finer points drawn by the coach on the whiteboard. His "attentional control" will determine if he can keep his focus, avoiding the defensive pressure from rattling him into a mistake or missed opportunity. His "working memory capacity" will be tested to not only hold on to the play call but the thousand other sub-skills that he requires to make it all work. The rate at which he can process this additional information and adjust on the fly will give his executive function time to complete the plan.

Cognitive scientists divide this process into two categories; domain-specific and domain-general abilities. In our point guard example, the basketball specific knowledge and skills are domain-specific while the underlying mental skills of attention, working memory, information processing and executive function are domain-general, used by the point guard in several facets of his life outside of basketball. We often use a computer metaphor, with software being the domain-specific, programmed instruction set and the hardware being the unique powers of the brain in each individual. This cognitive toolkit is assumed innate, handed down by parents, but research has found only about fifty percent of these abilities are inheritable.[10]

Another way to look at the software/hardware comparison is how researchers study athletes. For years, we studied athletes in their environment, comparing elite playmakers with newbies, known as the expert performance approach. Studies confirmed common sense that better players showed superior attention, memory, and processing speed when performing in their sport.

But what happens when you take the playmaker outside of her domain-specific world? Would they display better cognitive abilities than junior players in a generic setting? This observation, known as the cognitive components approach, tries to eliminate the "software" from the equation to see if playmakers bring advanced "hardware" to the table.

In 2010, University of Illinois researchers Michelle Voss and Arthur Kramer looked at twenty studies to determine if the cognitive components approach was valid. They found information processing speed in a general setting was a powerful indicator for success in sports, with the other abilities of attention, memory and executive function also showing a strong correlation. "Based on our results, there is a place for the cognitive component skills approach for extending current knowledge about how sport training affects the brain and acquisition of fundamental cognitive abilities."[11]

In 2019, similar results emerged from a meta-study completed by Hans-Erik Scharfen and Daniel Memmert at the German Sport University. They gathered 19 studies comparing the domain-general cognitive functions of elite versus non-elite athletes, in executive function, visual-perception and other functions.

"We found that high-performance level athletes do have superior cognitive functions compared with low-performance level athletes," they concluded. "Additionally, this knowledge could be used by coaches and scientists to test athletes not only physically but also on the cognitive domain and therefore further individualize training programs to enhance important cognitive functions and reduce (psychological) weaknesses to guarantee a holistic and sophisticated development of athletes."[12]

In several of these studies, working memory and executive function were broken down even further. Working memory control refers to the ability to manipulate the information in storage, organizing new input while discarding unneeded, old information. Working memory capacity, however, defines the amount of information that can be stored in the "episodic buffer", similar to the RAM of a computer. Higher capacity allows more information to be retained and processed by executive functions.

And speaking of executive function, experts split it into two categories; core executive function (CEF) and high executive function (HEF). CEF combines the base components of working memory, inhibition, and task-switching flexibility while HEF adds-on more advanced processes like planning, reasoning and problem-solving. Ultimately, executive function is the key hardware determinant of playmaker decision-making. This idea is not new to at least one German Bundesliga squad and their innovative sport psychologist.

Surrounded By The Helix

"All of the young players training with the seniors for the first time say the same thing: "Oh, that's fast!"[13] said Dr. Jan Mayer, managing director of TSG ResearchLab. After 13 years as the lead sport psychologist at parent club TSG Hoffenheim of the German Bundesliga, Mayer has seen hundreds of young soccer prospects develop in their youth academy with only the best playmakers rising to the senior team.

"Youth development must therefore follow one clear objective: Players need to learn to think very fast, consciously. On the pitch, they basically need to be on autopilot, like we are when driving a car, not deliberately thinking whether we're switching from second into third gear or how to operate the clutch. But pure instinct in itself is also no longer enough, as there's a match plan to implement. We want to speed up the processes inside the brain. Many athletes are too slow in that regard. But you can train and improve them,[14]"

While the club itself dates back over 120 years, the modern version of Hoffenheim formed in 1945. But they languished down in the fifth division of German soccer until Dietmar Hopp, billionaire and co-founder of SAP, the global software firm, gave their future a boost in 2000.

Determined to pull his hometown club out of obscurity, he invested heavily, especially in science, technology and facilities. Advancing steadily through the lower leagues, Hoffenheim advanced to the Bundesliga in 2008, the same year that Dr. Mayer joined the club. They stayed in the middle of the table for several years, no small feat for a recently promoted club, but then began their ascent in 2013 capped off with a third place finish in 2017-18 earning a ticket to the UEFA Champions League tournament.

Dr. Mayer's interest in technology as a training tool off the field created the most talked about facilities in world soccer. Hoffenheim was a pioneer of the Footbonaut, a 14 by 14 meter cage with 64 square targets, upper and lower, surrounding a player who stands in the middle. It launches a ball from one of four squares towards the player who then has to receive it, often with just two touches, redirect it to another square that has been lit up. It tracks time and accuracy and can increase difficulty as needed. Since 2014, Hoffenheim has used the system for all of its teams, from U12 to the professionals, one of only a handful of clubs in the world willing to pay the high price tag.

Similar tech-enabled tools populate the training facility, including a massive video wall on the team's practice pitch, used to show video game clips of their next opponent while Hoffenheim coaches teach tactics for the upcoming match. Video gaming is also a favorite of Dr. Mayer, despite critics who can't see the relevance. He emphasizes the power of thinking fast, "Improve the speed of information processing, the experience of changing objectives, monitoring objects. All of these things you need in the field can be improved by playing video games."[15] Partnering with a virtual reality software company, he sees it as another advantage that players can use without causing additional physical fatigue.

These overall test results add up to a key metric, the ExF score, tracked for all Hoffenheim players. Growing this measure gives the training a tangible goal that can compare players, assess new signings or young prospects, and report the progress being made from the technology investments.

"We are seeing lots of innovation now," said Dr. Mayer. "There are tracking devices showing you how fast and how far a player is running. We can analyze how many tackles and how many passes that a player makes. But all this data cannot explain successful soccer because it is missing information about what is going on inside the player.

There can be a physical reason a player is not sprinting so quickly or running as far, but there can also be a cognitive reason. Maybe he did not perceive the run quickly enough, maybe he was too slow to process the information to track the run."[16]

However, the crown jewel on the Hoffenheim campus is the Helix. Similar to the Footbonaut in its circular arena space, HD video displays and surround sound create a 360-degree environment. Newly upgraded in 2020 from a 180-degree first version, the Helix offers six different game modes that all require the player to use peripheral vision, attention to cues, multiple object tracking and reaction time - all aspects of executive function - to create hundreds of game-like decisions.

"It is a highly motivating environment in there, that is the idea," said Dr. Mayer. "Everyone in there should have fun. It is a really cool gaming environment, so the compliance is very high. You go in there and you play, you don't even know that you are training your executive functions."[17]

The question on the minds of coaches and front office administrators is the value for the investment. Can tracking and training executive function pay off in better players? A direct transfer of skill learned with technology to the actual sport domain has been an elusive result to prove. The number of dependent and independent variables to track is daunting, but Dr. Mayer takes a more philosophical stance.

"I don't think you can show directly that improvement in

the Helix arena will make them better players on the pitch. But my argument is always that as long as training in the gym is helpful for a player, then a cognitive training environment should be relevant as well. I don't know how much we will make them better, but if it is only a few percents, then we should do it."[18]

As a researcher at the German University for Prevention and Health Management in Saarbrücken, Dr. Mayer's work with Hoffenheim players offers a dual role to advance academic understanding of executive function (EF) especially in athletes. To help fellow coaches speed up the learning curve, Mayer and his associates, Jan Spielmann and Adam Beavan, penned a useful lessons-learned paper, published in the December 2019 edition of Frontiers in Psychology[19].

As they explain in the introduction, "During the planning and implementation of EF assessments, there are obstacles that may be encountered by practitioners and coaches throughout all levels of play (i.e., amateur to professional leagues), such as the choice of assessments, the financial and opportunity costs, how to convey the data into meaningful results to the team, and what assumptions can currently be made from the data that is supported by research.

By using the experience that we have gained by testing and training EFs for over 5 years at a professional 1st division football (Association Football) club in Germany, we aim to share our opinion on how to tackle these issues. We also aim to discuss the remaining barriers in EF research in hope of having more researchers and practitioners working together to collectively overcome them."

First, if a youth academy, club or sports organization were interested in assessing their players' EF, they should isolate by individual age groups (i.e., 11 years old, 12, 13, etc.). In another 2019 paper, the same trio of researchers plus others found that, "Overall, older athletes with more experience playing soccer had better EF than younger athletes. Furthermore, noticeable improvements in EF performance can also be observed with an increase of one year in age and playing experience during early adolescence. Thus, future studies should take caution when grouping players together with multiple birth years, especially in younger populations where the magnitude of change between ages are more prominent."

In fact, they dove deeper into the natural progression of EF during the adolescent years to find out if this growth in memory, inhibition and cognitive flexibility mirrored the general population of teenagers rather than the quantity and quality of sports participation. In other words, did nature or nurture grow a person's EF over time? It is an important question for coaches who see an opportunity to assess EF as a clever player selection tool; young players who test well in non-sport EF tasks may be genetically gifted with higher cognitive potential than their peers. Just like kids who mature physically at an earlier age, thus setting them up for better teams, better coaching and better long-term success, could a pre-teen who tests well on choice reaction, task switching and memory drills also surpass their age-matched competitors?

Thanks to their access to hundreds of soccer academy and senior team players at Hoffenheim, Dr. Mayer and his colleagues reviewed their data on 343 male players, ages 10-34, over three seasons. They tested them on four cognitive EF tasks; choice-reaction time, stop-signal reaction time, sustained attention and multiple object tracking. What they found was that performance on the tests matched a pattern seen in other research of a general population of similar ages. As age increased, EF went up.

So, what made the difference between elite players and average players? Perhaps something known as the "threshold effect", where some adolescent athletes reach a plateau, or threshold, of performance that lifts them into a higher class. Beyond that, there is no continued rise in generic EF superiority but a jump in sport-specific knowledge and experience.

As most athletes reach the age of maturity, about 20-22, they aren't getting "smarter" in a hardware sense but are getting upgraded software for their sport. And the researchers point that, "if the developmental trends reveal that EF performance begins to decrease when athletes are reaching the age where they become professional athletes, then the potential usefulness of assessing EFs for talent identification is questionable.

Accordingly, the use of EF assessments may be better

suited for the early detection of possible football players from a heterogenous cohort that does not yet play football at a high level or who has limited experience, rather than in the identification of the best performers in a homogenous cohort of high-level players."[20] Basically, EF assessment might be a great tool for finding the "needles in the haystack" of kids not playing sports but who have strong core abilities to succeed if they did.

And despite the high dollar investment that TSG Hoffenheim has made in cognitive assessment and training, in terms of staff and facilities, Dr. Mayer is transparently honest to not oversell the capabilities of his programs. He acknowledges that the jury is still out on the testing side of cognitive enhancement, "There remains a large debate on whether training with computer-based cognitive tasks can broadly transfer into real-world performances."[21] Balancing a young playmaker's time and the club's costs is the real world balancing act if coaches want to look into EF programs. Dr. Mayer suggests four subsets of players who may benefit the most from these activities.

"It is important that if clubs decide to invest in training EFs, the staff should further discuss both the financial cost of purchasing the equipment and the opportunity cost of spending the time and money on a different task. In order to reduce the opportunity cost, we emphasize the importance of cognitive training toward players who are: (i) regressing from their previous EF scores, (ii) wanting to engage in cognitive training, (iii) injured, and (iv) scoring in the lowest third within their age norms. The reason behind training players who performed in the lowest third is based on previous non-sporting literature reporting that a threshold effect may exist with natural abilities and expertise, where any improved ability beyond the requirement to compete at a high-level (i.e., the threshold) may not further improve performance. Contrastingly, this also means that players who are under the threshold may yield the potential to enhance their performance by improving their EFs."[22]

Fitness Bootcamp for the Brain

For many of us, one of the most anticipated, or dreaded, weeks in school gym class was the testing for the Presidential Fitness Test. By placing in the top 15% nationwide in all five of the strength, flexibility, agility and speed tests, you received a colorful cloth patch that Mom quickly sewed on to your backpack. Placing in the top 50% earned the National Fitness Award - still good but not as cool. And then there was the Participant patch, given to those who score in the lower 50 percent in one or more tests. For most kids, that patch usually went quickly into the trash can.

Interestingly, there was no similar set of tests for cognitive fitness. School itself was a test of knowledge and concepts, what psychology calls declarative knowledge. But unless a school offered standard intelligence (IQ) tests, which few rarely did, there was no index of the core thinking machinery that we have been discussing in this chapter, much like Hoffenheim is trying to measure EF. And the IQ measures have their own history of cultural bias. We need an alternative model, especially for fast-paced environments like sports, first responders and other high-stakes, high-pressure requirements.

It turns out that the Australian Army is also pursuing the same answers. They wanted to know the cognitive preparedness of their fighting force to respond to a conflict at a moment's notice. Their battlefield is drastically different from an athlete's but with a similar need to "train above the neck." So, they called on Dr. Eugene Aidman, a performance psychologist affiliated with the University of Sydney, the University of Newcastle and the Australian Defense Science and Technology Group.

"We study cognitive performance, in the lab and in the field, of both individuals and teams," said Dr. Aidman in an interview. "And more importantly, we study the cognitive fitness underpinning that."[23]

Just as with athletes, each soldier is a unique individual who brings a distinctive set of cognitive strengths and weaknesses to their job. Being able to assess and train these skills in a customized program is the mission of the Cognitive Gym, a set of mental exercises similar to a workout plan for the brain. It is the practical tool based on an overall framework that Dr. Aidman developed, which he calls the Cognitive Fitness Framework (CF2).

Using the gold standard processes of physical training, "isolate-overload-overrecover", the Cognitive Gym aims to improve "trainable cognitive primaries" like attention, executive control, task-switching and decision-making. Once deemed cognitively fit, a soldier advances to mission-ready training which includes tolerance to battle stresses like pain, sleep loss, surprise and uncertainty, and resistance to risks such as distraction, deception and manipulation.

While engaged in a mission, CF2 switches to operational performance issues like fatigue countermeasures, decision aids, and cognitive monitoring. Post-operation, the soldier engages in recovery modes of sleep monitoring, meditation, nutrition and social support.

"This is going to end up being the critical skill set for the solider of the future and within that decision-making space we're also beginning to work on their decision biases and their confidence calibration," said Dr. Aidman in an interview for the Defense Science and Technology Outlook.[24]

In a recent paper in Frontiers in Human Neuroscience, Dr. Aidman presented CF2 as a bridge between existing research in cognitive readiness (CR) and mental fitness (MF) to "examine these causal connections between CR and cognitive factors underpinning mental health to develop a more tractable and systemic approach to the assessment and training of high-performance cognition."[25]

In the race to find the perfect solution for soldiers, first-responders, or athletes, CF2 is a welcome top-down approach to outline not just the "how-to" but start first with the "what" and "why" of cognitive training. With many technology-driven apps in the marketplace that claim to increase an athlete's brain functioning, including useful transfer to their sport, the solutions are getting ahead of the research. We recommend that coaches and parents of developing athletes always ask these app vendors for the peer-reviewed research that shows how their training technology has specifically improved the underlying cognitive skills in their sport.

In fact, Dr. Aidman labels CF2 as a "working hypothesis mapping out the research agenda to identify and measure key attributes of CF, underpinning both real-time cognitive performance under challenging conditions and the resilience that enables career longevity and lifelong thriving."

Despite the progress made to understand a potential playmaker's cognitive fingerprint, they are still human, susceptible to good days and bad days, boosted and bruised egos, and the thrill of victory and the agony of defeat. In other words, athletes have emotions that directly affect their decision-making performance. In the next chapter, let's find out more about how feelings fill up our focus, working memory and choices.

3

EMOTION

"Sports is like rock 'n' roll. Both are dominant cultural forces, both speak an international language, and both are all about emotions."

— Phil Knight

Let's revisit that NCAA football championship game between Alabama and Georgia. Late in the third quarter, with Alabama still trailing by ten points, Mekhi Brown, a Crimson Tide linebacker and special teams player, took a right-handed swipe at a Georgia player after a punt play ended in a minor skirmish. The referee flagged him fifteen yards for unsportsmanlike conduct, not helping his team's field position. Coach Saban gave him an earful on the sideline, to which Brown listened but said nothing. Then, a few seconds later, Brown yelled back at Kerry Stevenson, Alabama's director of player development, and appeared to reach around a teammate to shove him.[1] Players and coaches stepped in and redirected Brown over to the bench to cool off. The TV cameras caught it all, beaming the awkward altercation to millions of fans around the world. In Coach Saban's world of discipline and order, this was a surprising breach of emotional control.

Ten minutes later, Brown dashed downfield to make a spectacular tackle on a kickoff play. He knew he needed to atone for his earlier mistake. In the post-game, winning locker room, Brown was immediately contrite about his outburst, "I really felt like a jerk. That's not how I am. I wanted to win, that's what it was. I did something stupid. I could have cost us the game."

"I'm a grown man. I knew I had to make a big play to get my guys to wake up. That's what I did. That's definitely out of my character what I did. I knew I had to keep my composure and poise. I could have affected the whole team, and I didn't want to do that."[2]

As we know, hindsight is always in focus. But despite the teachings of Saban, a Hall of Fame coach, a player still made an emotional decision, out of character and out of line. What happened? Excusing those conscious decisions with throwaway lines, blaming "the heat of the moment" or "his emotions got the best of him" does nothing to help prevent it from happening in the next game.

Clearly, human decisions are influenced if not sometimes controlled by adrenaline, ego, confidence and anger. Learning how to identify and check them before it's too late is often a missed coaching opportunity. But to teach control in stressful situations requires an understanding of how athletes behave differently when the stakes are high. Every player brings in their own smorgasbord of feelings into a game, stirs them up on the field with competitive fire, bringing them to a boil. What should be logical, tactical decisions often become reactionary impulses that cause smart players to do "something stupid."

Grace Under Pressure

When researching these topics, athletes in individual sports, like tennis, golf, and gymnastics, are less complicated to study than players in team sports, due to the reduced number of variables. Watching a pro golfer melt down on the back nine to give up a lead is not only uncomfortable to watch but also instructive, as he can only blame himself.

But watching the Atlanta Falcons blow a 25-point third quarter lead to the New England Patriots in Super Bowl LI was a team catastrophe. Picking out individual contributions to the collapse is harder to do. In both cases, there seems to be a "snowball rolling downhill" effect as one poor play leads to deeper despair which only raises anxiety, resulting in the next negative outcome. Commonly referred to as "choking," when a player performs well below expectations based on past performances, the symptoms are obvious while the cause needs more explanation.

Enter Dr. Michael Eysenck, emeritus professor in psychology at Royal Holloway, University of London, and Dr. Mark Wilson, professor of performance psychology at the University of Exeter. Together, they developed the Attentional Control Theory - Sports (ACTS), which was an outcrop of the foundational Attentional Control Theory which can apply to a wide variety of domains.

"Sport provides an almost perfect environment for examining performance under pressure. Skills that have been honed and perfected during practice can break down just when the need to execute them is greatest. In studying this paradoxical effect, Baumeister defined pressure as 'any factor or combination of factors that increase the importance of performing well.' The proposed mechanism by which pressure exerts its effect on skilled performance is via increased anxiety, an emotional response to threat, comprising cognitive worry and physiological arousal," wrote Eysenck and Wilson, et al.[3]

Ah yes, "cognitive worry and physiological arousal," also known by coaches as "loading your shorts." Players who panic in the moment either take a very conservative next action, try something well beyond their abilities or simply freeze. According to ACTS, this pressure-performance influence is bidirectional, leading to the familiar downward spiral of mental mistakes following initial errors.

At its core, the overarching ACT suggests there are two systems of attention:

- A goal-direction attention that focuses on top-down objectives like score a goal, earn a shutout, or win the game.

- A stimulus-driven attention that reacts to bottom-up sensory information during the game (the "shiny object" distraction that does not serve the top-down goals).

In addition, ACT states that working memory plays a vital part in how anxiety affects performance. Specifically, the central executive function of the brain, an amalgam of working memory and attention, that controls our planning, logic and decision-making. This includes three sub-systems:

- Inhibition which prevents our attention being controlled by task-irrelevant stimuli that doesn't serve our purposes (like trash talk from an opponent, thinking about the last three missed shots, etc.)

- Shifting, which manages the allocation of attention to multiple, simultaneous tasks (monitoring the defender near you, looking downfield for a pass, listening to a teammate, etc.)

- Updating controls working memory capacity, deleting old information when new stimuli arrive (that shot attempt has passed, so I need new opportunities)

ACT deals with the first two executive functions, inhibition and shifting. "In regard to ACT and its implications for decision-making in pressurized environments, we can state that anxiety reduces the efficiency of both the inhibition function (negative attentional control) and the shifting function (positive attentional control), in effect making an individual more distractible," explains Wilson, et al.[4]

But then how are playmakers different? Do they process pressure-packed moments differently than everyone else? Yes they do, according to Eysenck, Wilson and ACTS. Two cognitive biases come into play, attentional and interpretive. A player with an attentional bias will place more emphasis on threat-related events, spending any available working memory on the negative cues (a turnover they just caused, an opponent playing really well, etc.)

If they have an interpretive bias, they will translate neutral information threateningly because of past errors. Instead of seeing the next situation logically and objectively, they assume it will end badly ("I've missed my last three shots, so now every shot looks harder"). In addition, ACTS also predicts that players calculate both the potential, perceived costs of their mistakes and the likely probability of losing because of those mistakes.

Consider a soccer defender who commits an own goal, knocking the ball into his own net. The cost of the mistake is significant, as he perceives it, but if it happened late in the second half to give the other team a lead, then the probability of his team losing for his mistake also increases. Contrast that event with earlier in the game, when he made a wayward pass to a teammate in the center of the field. The intercepted pass did not lead to anything negative. The cost of the error, perceived as minor, did not change the probability of losing the game, at least in the defender's mind.

The playmaker, however, does not fall for these biases, seeing the field with less emotion and worry, able to shrug off any past mistakes. Because of this emotional control, they can keep their attention and working memory laser focused on the top-down, goal-directed mission of the overall game.

Anxiety in the NFL

With their new ACTS framework developed, Eysenck and Wilson wanted to put it out into the real world to test its validity. Specifically, does the dependence of current actions on past mistakes really affect outcomes, and is that dependence heightened by a high-pressure situation? Testing athletes in lab-created settings does not really offer the same adrenaline-pumping scenarios as an actual game in front of thousands of fans.

Yet, most coaches will prohibit doing psychological research on players during a competitive match. So, joined by their colleagues, David Harris and Sam Vine, Eysenck and Wilson dug into the massive game dataset of the NFL.

How massive, you ask? They extracted every single offensive play from every game for the 2009 to 2016 seasons - 212,356 plays, to be exact.

"Based on the predictions of ACTS, it was hypothesized that there would be: an increased probability of play failure on high pressure plays; an increased probability of one play failure following another (i.e., dependence); and an additional interactive effect, such that the negative effect of negative performance feedback would be exacerbated when pressure is already high," wrote the researchers.[5]

With the help of six experienced, college football coaches, they defined an offensive play failure as either a loss of possession, (a fumble or interception), or a lack of forward progress (an incomplete pass, or a tackle behind the line of scrimmage, including a sack). A pressure situation included a cumulative 6 point (0-5) rating based on if the play was third or fourth down; the game score was within 8 points (one TD and a 2-point conversion); it was the fourth quarter; the offensive team was behind and had the ball; and they were in the "red zone," inside their opponent's 20-yard line.

The research team plowed through the data set (with help from computational tools), finding pressure situations, then observing the play sequence. They confirmed their first two hypotheses, as expected, that high-pressure situations caused, on average, more failed plays and that a failed play was most likely followed by another unsuccessful play. But what was interesting to support ACTS was that the combination of the two, pressure and failure, increased the likelihood of a streak of negative plays.

"Not only does prior failure increase the chance of further failure, but this effect is larger under increasing levels of situational pressure," they concluded. "Indeed, at the highest levels of pressure (i.e., a pressure score of 4 or 5) there is a 50% probability that one failure will be followed by another, compared to only a 27% probability at low levels of pressure (i.e., a pressure score of 1),"[6]

ACTS predicts this result, as the increased pressure causes a rise in the perceived cost of failure while a bad play will raise the perception of the probability of losing. Cognitive anxiety goes up and false, distracting clues fill the player's attention and working memory.

Eysenck and Wilson believe that this is how playmakers distinguish themselves. "Performers who can forget their mistakes (or good plays from opponents) — especially when pressure is heightened — are less likely to feel anxious and experience the disruption of attentional control associated with choking. It may be that this is a key characteristic of performers who are described as clutch under pressure. Second, practitioners seeking to help performers deal more effectively in pressure situations could use ACTS to guide intervening at two stages; first by reducing the likelihood that environmental pressure leads to anxiety, or second, by limiting anxiety-induced impairments to effective attention control."[7]

In fact, having a short-term memory is almost a cliche

among football cornerbacks. Even the best will occasionally get beat by a wide receiver for a long pass or touchdown, with their mistake being seen by thousands in the stadium, if not millions on TV. While they try to identify and remember how they lost the one versus one battle, the disappointment, either as an attentional or interpretive bias, cannot linger long in their memory. Otherwise, as Eysenck and Wilson have shown, the next play could be worse.

Veteran NFL coach Jim Schwartz, now the defensive coordinator of the Philadelphia Eagles, knows the importance of dismissing blown plays, not to forget the lesson learned but to clear the mind for the next play. After a tough loss to the Minnesota Vikings in 2019, where his cornerbacks gave up 333 passing yards and four touchdowns, he said, "I don't know that any of those were lack of confidence or [not] putting a play behind them, but whether it was a penalty, whether it was a physical error or a technique error or a communication error, another bad play ended up rolling up on them and that's the life they live. It's just what we deal with, and corners need to be able to put bad plays behind them, and we've been inconsistent doing that."[8]

These research results are not exclusive to football. In a 2011 data review, Zheng Cao et al. found that the free-throw percentage of NBA players went down significantly in the last seconds of high-pressure games.[9] Daniel Link and Sebastian Wenninger examined data from elite level beach volleyball matches, including Olympic matches, from 2012 to 2016 to see if losing one side-out point typically leads to a second side-out failure.

Indeed, there were significantly more errors by a team, on average, after a previous point loss. Even at this level of sport, the power of anxiety and confidence has an effect.

"Clearly, it is also the goal of every player to act as variably and unpredictably as possible. The elite athletes in the sample are at the level they are because they are able to put this into practice. Elite players must also have a high mental performance and stability, which reduces effects of failure. Nevertheless, sequence effects in beach volleyball are found, which support the existence of psychological momentum in this sport," wrote Link and Wenninger.[10]

King Roger and the Spoiled Prince

Sitting on a snowy embankment at the bottom of a frozen waterfall in the Swiss Alps, Bear Grylls asked Roger Federer a question that he probably knew the answer to. "So, did you have, like, your Roger Federer cool temperament when you were a kid?" Federer smiled sheepishly and replied, "Not so much. I was the opposite of cool. I had a big temper back in the day and it took me a long time to figure it out."[11]

For those that did not follow Federer's youth career, it may surprise that the stoic King Roger, winner of a record

20 Grand Slam singles titles, was once a hothead. "He used to not be a role model," said Marco Chiudinelli, a Swiss player and friend of Federer's since the age of 6.[12]

His talent was apparent, but his future was unsure because of his inability to control his outbursts. Taylor Dent beat a 15-year-old Federer in a juniors match back in 1996. "Watching him in the juniors and early on in the pros, he definitely had a tendency to let his emotions overwhelm him in a negative way," said Dent. "When things weren't going his way, he had a tendency to hang his head and just have a negative attitude going on."[13]

Federer told Grylls, as part of a 2018 episode on his Running Wild adventure series, about a time when he was 16 and lost his cool during a practice match at the National Tennis Center, with a newly installed court backdrop, only to have Federer launch his tennis racket at it after losing a point. "That thing went like a knife through butter," said Federer with a smirk. His coach immediately kicked him off the court, and he had to clean toilets for the next week at the Center to help pay for his damages.

After almost two years of searching for ways to manage the ups and downs of seeking perfection in his tennis career, Federer settled on a balance of fire and ice. "You know like, have the fire and desire to win but the icy coolness to absorb losses and absorb bad mistakes."[14]

Being able to find peace while competing, to avoid the attentional and interpretive biases of distractions on the court, was the perfect pairing to his well-practiced technical skills. "Previously I always thought it was just tactical and technique, but every match has become almost mental and physical. I try to push myself not to get upset and stay positive, and that's what my biggest improvement is over all those years. Under pressure I can see things very clear," he said. "Once you find that peace, that place of peace and quiet, harmony and confidence, that's when you start playing your best."[15]

Inspiring words from the greatest tennis player of all-time, but let's dive into more research specifically designed to test a tennis player's cognitive decision-making skill. Earlier, we learned that anxiety can cause athletes to focus more on bottom-up stimuli at the expense of top-down tactical goals. We also know that an athlete, let's say a tennis player in this case, gathers environmental cues from two sources, kinematic (the bodily movements of opponents) and contextual (knowledge gained from a prior study of the opponent combined with the current state of the match, including score, set, and tactics). We associate this contextual knowledge with top-down, logical thinking while we link the kinematic cues to bottom-up attention. But in shorter lab-based experiments, this long-term contextual knowledge never emerges.

So, as ACTS has proposed, if anxiety causes a switch to bottom-up attention, then an inexperienced tennis player will lose the advantages of match-based contextual information when making shot by shot decisions. Expert players, like Roger Federer, who can manage their reaction to adversity will use both the contextual and kinematic data that is available, thanks to an attentional control system that can stand up to adversity.

Back in 2015, four sport science researchers at Brunel University in London designed an experiment to answer this very question. Adam Cocks and Daniel Bishop who, with David Broadbent, run the Learning, Expertise, Action, and Perception (LEAP) Lab, joined Robin Jackson (now with Loughborough University) and Mark Williams (now at the University of Utah) to test one of the prime tenets of ACTS.

They recruited 24 tennis players, 12 players rated highly by the British Tennis Membership Rating, and 12 players who were less skilled. On a large video screen, the players watched film of 48 match situations from a first-person perspective. Through editing software, they manipulated the scenes to show just three; with only kinematic close-ups of the opponent across the net, with only the court markings and just animated cylinders representing the players (no kinematic info), and finally, the entire scene with the opponent and all the court details. The players had to predict where oncoming shots would land and then report on the level of mental effort they spent in doing so. This provided a score of not only positional accuracy, but the processing efficiency of their decisions.

To add stress to the exercise, the players were told that national team coaches would watch their performance, and they placed a video camera behind the players to capture their movements. They were also told, falsely, that their performance was below expectations for their current rating and they needed to show a 10% improvement to hold their place.

The results did not disappoint. As the four researchers wrote in their paper, "anxiety was shown to impact the ability of skilled performers to use contextual information, suggesting that anxiety may have impacted more greatly on the processing of high-level, rather than low-level, cognitive processes. In line with the propositions of ACT, the reduced ability to use such top-down information may be due to a prioritization of the stimulus driven attentional system."[16]

Three years later, in 2018, Bishop, Williams and Broadbent were back again with a similar study involving soccer players. This time they focused on just the relationship between anxiety and contextual priors, the learned knowledge about an opponent's habits, tendencies and the specific game scenario. Does a player like to shoot with her right or left foot? Are they aggressive on the attack or play more defensively? How do these habits change based on the score and time left in the game? As they questioned with tennis, will stress affect the accuracy and/or the efficiency of their soccer decisions for their experience level?

Twelve expert (over ten years of experience) soccer players were asked to view life-size video of oncoming attackers with the ball. When the scene occluded, they asked the players to predict if the opponent would cut left or right. They did this task under four different scenarios involving contextual priors and anxiety. First, in a low anxiety state and with no contextual information, then adding stress to the situation with the knowledge of video recording and coach evaluations, as in their tennis experiment.

Next, the researchers informed the players of tendencies that this video opponent had, such as the percentage of time they preferred one direction over another. Then they manipulated this set-up with low and high anxiety states.

The researchers wanted to find out if the storage of contextual information in working memory, along with the added resources necessary to manage a stressful situation, would cause a drop in either performance accuracy or processing efficiency or both. A soccer player whose right foot is dominate will often prefer to cut to her right to allow her stronger foot to shoot. While this tendency, or contextual prior, is a preference, it is not always true. They hypothesized that playmakers can hold this clue in their working memory while also monitoring the real-time kinematic information in front of them, like the angle of the hips.

Sure enough, they confirmed that for these experienced playmakers the added anxiety does lower processing efficiency, but with added contextual prior information, there is no compound effect on performance or efficiency. "It appears that contextual information and anxiety influence performance through different mechanisms and impact attentional resources independent of each other."[17] While this experiment did not include a control group of novice players, this breakthrough finding takes us another step forward in understanding how the best players manage stress while also taking advantage of all available information.

Also in 2018, Mark Williams teamed up with Oliver Runswick and Andre Roca to test cricket batters under stress. Again, they wondered about the effects of loading working memory with not only anxiety but also situational context info. Using eye tracking, they noticed that batters under stress use more gaze fixations of shorter duration to more focus points than under low stress that resulted in fewer good bat-ball contacts. But the contextual information did not affect performance in the same way as anxiety.

"Situation-specific context affected performance and behavioral measures but not anxiety, cognitive load or perceptual cognitive processes, suggesting that performance is influenced through different mechanisms from anxiety that are independent of working memory load."[18]

The Stillness of Stoicism

After beating the Milwaukee Bucks for the third straight time in the 2019 NBA Eastern Conference Finals, the Toronto Raptors led the series three games to two, just one game away from reaching the NBA Finals. Their laconic superstar, Kawhi Leonard, was asked "how do you beat the

Bucks four times in a row?" by TNT reporter Kristen Ledlow. In a demeanor that was neither dismissive nor sarcastic, Leonard answered in a monotone, "I don't know. I haven't done it. We're taking it one game at a time." Not to be denied, Ledlow pressed on with a follow-up, "With you one win away from a trip to the NBA Finals, what's this team's mentality with history on the line?" With nothing but sincerity on his face, Leonard responded, "I mean, I haven't even gotten to the locker room yet. We just finished the game."[19]

After learning at the feet of the master of logic-based, unemotional answers, Spurs coach Gregg Popovich, for seven seasons, including the 2014 NBA Championship, Leonard focuses only on what's in front of him without the burden of what-if scenarios, either forward or backward looking. As Popovich succinctly described him, "He loves the game," Popovich continues. "He ignores the rest of it."[20]

Ignores the rest of it. That is exactly what it means to control your attention by acknowledging anxiety but ignoring its flashing lights. Stay in the moment, as the Stoics would say. In fact, the link between stoicism, the Greek philosophy of self-virtue, and playmakers like Leonard is almost cliche. As a "person who represses feelings or endures patiently," (the common definition of stoic), Leonard guards against the endless barrage of distractions both on the court and off. "I don't like to bring attention to myself," he admits. "I don't like to make a scene."[21]

It's difficult to peer inside the mind of a stoic playmaker, thanks to their economy of words and emotions. They brush aside questions and issues that seem to matter to others as superfluous to the core mission, whatever that is. After moving from San Antonio to the colder climate of Toronto, a reporter asked a lighthearted question about enduring the long winters. Again, without a smirk, Leonard tried to not only understand the question but answer it earnestly. "I just wear a jacket. We're in buildings a lot. We're not outside playing in the snow. It's some good scenery."[22]

As the slave turned philosopher Epictetus said 2,000 years ago, "In life our first job is this, to divide and distinguish things into two categories: externals I cannot control, but the choices I make with regard to them I do control. Where will I find good and bad? In me, in my choices."[23]

Ryan Holiday resurrected the ancient writings of Marcus Aurelius, Seneca and Epictetus in his bestselling books on stoicism. In fact, dozens of elite playmakers and coaches cite his first book of a trilogy on the topic, The Obstacle Is The Way, as a method to quiet the noise of stress in their heads so they can focus their attention, working memory and executive function solely on the objective in front of them.

"Stoicism is the distinction between what you can control and what you can't," Holiday said. "That's probably the hardest idea of pro sports—that you have to detach yourself from the results and focus exclusively on what you do and do it well. You can't get mad about missing the shot, or losing a game, or calls that went against you. You have to focus on what you were supposed to do and whether you did it right."[24]

An early fan of Holiday's writing and a student of high performance techniques, Tim Ferriss, bestselling author and podcast host, also cites the philosophy as a natural tonic for not only superstars but also developing playmakers. "In sports, failure is the nature of the beast," he said. "It's what separates the also-rans from champions, especially being able to come back from a mistake and be better rather than hesitant. For the best athletes, the obstacles shaped them. They have an operating system. They are resilient."[25]

Leonard and the Raptors won the 2019 NBA Finals, four games to two over the Golden State Warriors, bringing the city of Toronto its first championship since 1993 when the Blue Jays won the World Series. When asked to compare the joy of that moment with the pain of losing his father to a murderer's bullet at 16, he responded, "It just gave me a sense and feel that life and basketball are two different things and just really enjoy your time and moments."

Fellow NBA All-Star CJ McCollum is also a disciple of stoicism, specifically the concept of apatheia, the state of being free from emotional disturbance. "I live with the result, man," McCollum said. "I know who I am. I know what I can be out there. I have confidence in myself. I don't get discouraged over a few poor shooting nights. I don't get overly excited over a few great shooting nights."[26]

There is no sign that Kawhi Leonard has ever read a word of the Stoic masters. But how he carries himself through life reflects the philosophy and its usefulness. Of course, being 6'7" with a 7'2" wingspan helps in the NBA, but how many other players have even more impressive physical gifts that have not become a two-time NBA Finals MVP? The thousands of decisions he makes in every game are unburdened by extraneous, attention-grabbing thoughts. But that skill is not something that can be turned on when the whistle blows and stored away at the end of the game, returning to a life crowded with worry and anxiety. It is a lifestyle that provides benefits in both directions.

"You know, I'll never try to win an award," said Leonard. "I'm out there just playing for my team. If I get noticed for my individual performance, that's what happens. Other than that, I'm just trying to win the game."[27]

As legendary Sports Illustrated writer, Lee Jenkins, opened his 2016 exploration of Kawhi, "His name evokes an island, warm and remote, enchanting and unspoiled.[28]"

Undoubtedly, a peaceful place to make decisions.

Waiting for Enough

"It all started back when I was 13. I wanted to become tougher. There was something missing. My physical game was getting better, my mental game was good enough. But there was something missing mentally that I knew would take me to another level. So, I asked my dad, 'can you make me tougher to compete against these kids who were older.'"[29] That is where the legend of Tiger Woods, the competitor, began. His dad, the late Earl Woods, agreed to use tactics similar to his US Army Green Beret psychological training he learned in Vietnam.

"He would get so angry with me. He would look at me and grit his teeth. But he wasn't permitted to say a word, except for one word. And that word was the release word," said Mr. Woods. Becoming an inside joke to both of them, known as the E-word, Tiger could utter "enough" when he wanted the abuse to stop. It started with simple distractions, like Earl dropping his golf bag during Tiger's backswing or tossing a bucket of balls at him while putting. Then, as Tiger learned to cope with these simple focus killers, the verbal abuse began, being called vulgar names with racial slurs.

"What made it more frustrating was that I knew what he was doing, and I still couldn't stop the frustration. I couldn't handle it. But then I would get a bigger tolerance over time. He would never push me over the edge. He would take me right up to the breaking point then back off. Eventually it would take more and more and more, to the point where it didn't bother me anymore."

"And finally, I said, 'Tiger, your training is over. I promise that you'll never meet another person as mentally tough as you in your entire life," said the elder Woods. "And he hasn't, and he never will."

With this new sense of invincibility, Tiger learned that only he would control the ultimate height of his game. "There was always another level to attain. The more you learn the game, the more you're aware of these other levels. It's a never-ending struggle because you can always get better. It's a journey where there's no arrival, and that's the beauty of it."[30]

When his dad passed away in 2006, Tiger Woods' life unraveled. Through a well-documented series of self-destruction ending in an SUV crash outside his home, the winner of 82 PGA events and 15 Major tournaments faced a daily barrage of verbal and written criticisms, abuse and dire predictions about his future. Now, he had to use the apatheia training from his teens to silence the voices all around him. "Did they think they could get to me? They couldn't," he wrote. "I saw but didn't see, I heard but didn't hear."[31]

In his 2017 book, Tiger credited this unusual father-son training for his success. "The psychological training that my father used inured me to whatever I might have to deal with in golf. The most important thing I learned was that anybody could say whatever they wanted, but I ultimately had control over how I reacted."

"My father's approach was what I needed, and it worked for me. Maybe it would be called 'tough love' now, but it went a long way towards making me the golfer I was becoming as a junior and an amateur."

Recalling his first win at Augusta in 1997, he wrote, "It especially [helped] when I walked that short distance from the ninth green to the tenth tee after shooting 40. None of this was in my mind then, but I've been convinced for a long time that had Pop not trained me as he had, I could have easily crumbled after how I started the Masters. I could have panicked, and who knows what would have been going through my mind as I approached the tenth tee and what would prove to be the pivotal shot in my young professional career."[32]

Live Fire Training

Some parents and coaches will undoubtedly look at the Woods training regimen as cruel and over the line. The surrender word was always available to use if the pressure was too much. The difference with Tiger and Earl is just that, it is a father-son relationship that can be fragile at best and life-altering at worst. Just Google "bad sports parent behavior" and dozens of upsetting examples of overzealous moms and dads will show just how warped our youth sports world can get.

Even the well-intentioned promotion of a child's sporting ability can be too much. When a two-year-old

Tiger appeared on the Mike Douglas Show with his dad to show off his fledgling golf skills to an amused audience, not all the guests approved. Jimmy Stewart, the legendary actor, was also a guest on the show with Bob Hope. Afterwards, Stewart said to Douglas backstage, "I've seen too many precious kids like this sweet little boy, and too many starry-eyed parents."[33]

While we, as authors, do not directly endorse this form of "mental training," we know that coaches have long used "pressure training" and "planned distractions" as strategies for building an athlete's resilience. So much so that a fair amount of research has looked at the effectiveness of these methods for developing playmakers. Let's look at two recent studies.

First, a guided interview by three Dutch researchers from Vrije Universiteit[34] with nine talent development and high-performance coaches involved in both individual and team Olympic sports, including golf, archery, track and field, fencing, field hockey, triathlon and baseball. The researchers asked about both the planned disruptions used but also their desired outcomes from this training. They identified nine different types, each with their own sub-types:

- **Location**: Coaches would deliberately choose poor travel accommodations to introduce the stress of poor sleep, jet lag, long travel delays, etc. As one coach described, "On our way to the quarter final [of a minor tournament], we simulated the bus having a failure. I thought it was necessary for them to experience such things... So about one kilometer from the stadium we told them the bus broke down. The bus driver was playing it perfectly as well. And we just stood back to see how they would handle this."

- **Competition simulation**: By creating a structure of tournament competitors and conditions, coaches sought to learn about their athletes when faced with the pressure of the big moment. "They have to shoot 72 arrows against each other [in a tournament format]. They know who they have to compete against. Know each other's scores. So, they know how much they would need to shoot in order to advance to the next round."

- **Punishments and rewards**: the coaches debated the use of a stick and carrot approach with some using physical punishment like push-ups or running while others used more task-based punishments like cleaning up the gym or cooking dinner for their teammates if they did not perform well. For rewards, playing time, both in practice and in games, was the prize. "They have to compete in small games during practice against a direct competitor and the person who wins plays the next game"

- **Physical strain**: Surprise use of especially hard training sessions to judge an athlete's resolve with no time to mentally prepare was a common tactic mentioned by the coaches. "Train extremely hard. At 110%, 120% taxation. Just make it really tough. Then you see who is able to really push their boundaries"

- **Stronger competition**: At more elite levels, athletes often get complacent winning every match. Coaches need to challenge them with stronger opponents which teaches them there is, as Tiger said, always another level above. "In [their own country] they don't have any competition. With those athletes, you have to go to competitions abroad. Let them struggle a bit there. Just so they realize they still have a long way to go."

- **Distractions**: The domain of Earl Woods, coaches would use both sound and physical distractions to throw off the rhythm of their athletes. Piping in loud crowd noise into a scrimmage or unexpected obstructions work well. "During penalty corners we would throw balls at the players to get them out of their concentration. And you notice this causes some stress."

- **Unfairness**: Life isn't fair and the sooner that athletes adjust to what's out of their control helps them internalize their environment. "We would tell referees to favor one or disadvantage the other... those kinds of things we try to integrate in practice and that makes it very difficult for [the athletes]."

- **Restrictions**: Limit their game in a way that throws the athletes out of their comfort zone, like making them wear earplugs so they can't communicate with each other. "To simulate the European Championship–small stadium, a lot of people — you cannot hear anything, you can't hear each other, can't give directions to each other."

When the researchers asked the coaches what they hoped to accomplish from these distractions, four major goals emerged:

- **Familiarization**: Anxiety is part of sports, so athletes need to recognize it and learn to deal with it. "Stress exists. We have a tendency to be afraid of it. To not talk about it. To say as long as you remain focused on your task, everything will be fine. But I believe by not facing it, you are just making it bigger... My approach was to say 'guys we are going to be confronted with situations that are going to be uncomfortable. How can we prepare ourselves for that as best as possible?'... So we tried to become comfortable in uncomfortable situations. That was my starting point."

- **Creating awareness**: Once an athlete experiences stress, what do they learn from it? "we look for ways to give them insights into their own behavior. First, they need insight, only then they can start working with it. Constantly expose people to situations, in a lot of different ways both inside and outside sports, that every time again exposes behavior."

- **Develop and refine personal resources**: Given their familiarity and awareness of their weaknesses under pressure, what can they do about it. "They have to learn to stay in the moment. They have to learn to become aware of whether they are thinking about what happened or thinking about their score, and they have to get back to the here and now. Through meditation and breathing exercises. Visualization, routines, pre-shot routines. It can teach them to stand on their own two legs. To encourage them to try and find their own solutions. Make them more self-reliant. In that way they are going to have a much bigger chance to make it, rather than when everything is being done for them."

- **Promote team processes**: The planned disruptions can be a tool that players used to learn to trust each other, especially in team sports. "I have a leadership group and from time to time I throw in some tension for them. Look there are several people in this group, but each person has its role ... And we can use this tension to test these roles."[35]

In the other 2020 study, researchers from the University of Essex and Sheffield Hallam University conducted a meta-analysis of fourteen existing papers, with ten in sport and four in law enforcement including almost 400 athletes or officers, on the success of pressure training (PT) as it relates to performance in a real setting.

Also called acclimatization training or anxiety training, PT's aim is to increase perceived pressure during training to raise performance levels of athletes during actual competition. Interestingly, PT can ramp up with tougher demands during drills or harsher consequences of poor performance, although consequences, like monetary rewards or fines, playing time, and coach evaluations, seem to produce better results.

Regardless of the form of PT used, they must deliver it during technical play, so that the athlete can learn to execute skills with the added layer of stress. As we saw with ACTS, managing the distractions and their biases is the aim to playmaking skills.

"PT does not just train the ability to cope with anxiety;

instead, it trains the ability to cope while simultaneously executing skills or making decisions," the authors write. "PT is not necessarily a separate exercise from a performer's normal training regimen because a coach or instructor can increase pressure during an already scheduled exercise. For instance, if a basketball team already practices free throws, then practicing free throws under pressure does not necessarily take much more time. Therefore, PT enhances existing training rather than introducing a completely new and unfamiliar exercise."[36]

Across the fourteen studies, including novice and experienced participants, PT did significantly improve later performance when compared to control groups who did not receive PT. Since the control groups still practiced as long as the test group, the takeaway for coaches is that layering PT on top of normal practice plans will reap benefits without adding more time.

"Coaches or instructors could consider introducing appropriate amounts of pressure early in a learner's development," the researchers concluded. "PT's effectiveness for novices illustrates that individuals might not have to master a skill before training it under pressure. Furthermore, when learners train while feeling emotions of competition, they may be more engaged and also discover the emotions, thoughts, and behavior that they need to perform optimally."[37]

CJ McCollum knows that stoicism's lessons on managing

external sources of anxiety will carry him forward to meet the demands of the NBA.

"That sense of Stoicism really kind of resonated with me to where I was like, Wow, this is something I can practice. I can practice steadiness. I can practice accepting things I cannot change. I can practice a certain calmness, a certain coolness, an understanding of how to really just be content with what I have. Understanding that there are certain things that I may yearn for but it may not be great for me. Understanding that certain failures are going to help shape me and make me into a better person to where I won't be afraid of those failures."[38]

PART II

CONSTRAINTS

4

TIME

"We didn't lose the game, we just ran out of time."

— Vince Lombardi

One and a half seconds remained on the clock. Needing two points to tie and three to win, the University of Virginia Cavaliers would inbound the ball in their offensive half against a stingy Auburn University Tiger defense that had held them ten points below their season average.

The referee handed the ball to Ty Jerome, point guard and future first-round NBA draft pick, and began the five-second countdown. With the clock starting as soon as they touched the ball, Virginia would have no time to pass but just catch and shoot. Virginia's sharpshooter guard, Kyle Guy, Mr. Indiana Basketball in his high school days, broke through the pack of players in the free throw lane and headed for the near corner. Jerome fired the ball to him. Pivoting on the spot, Guy leaped into a three-point jump shot with eight-tenths of a second remaining. Just before the ball bounced off the side of the rim, a referee's whistle pierced through the noise of over 72,000 fans at US Bank Stadium in downtown Minneapolis.

Samir Doughty, Auburn's leading scorer that night who had chased Guy across the floor, jumped up to block the shot but his momentum carried him into Guy bumping the shooter as he released the ball, resulting in a three-shot foul. The Sacramento Kings draft pick made all three free throws to give Virginia a one point lead. Now with six-tenths of a second left in the game, Auburn's Bryce Brown caught a desperation full-court pass at the opposite free throw line. Like Guy, he spun off one foot to get a shot off before time expired, but the ball fell short ending the game and sending Virginia to the 2019 National Championship game to face the Texas Tech University Red Raiders.

As predicted by the media pundits, the title game went down to the last minute, with the Cavaliers' De'Andre Hunter making a corner three with 12.9 seconds left to tie the game. After bringing the ball up the court, Auburn's Jarrett Culver's three-point shot attempt rattled off the rim and off of a Virginia player, giving possession back to the Tigers with 0.8 seconds remaining.

But this time, it was Virginia who had to stop a last-second shot to avoid crashing out of the tournament. In an almost identical set-up to the closing second of the semi-final game, Auburn in-bounded the ball in front of their own bench to Culver who pivoted in the corner but the Virginia defender, Braxton Key, jumped to the side of Culver and blocked the shot to send the game to overtime. From there, Virginia took control and won their first national championship in school history.

Two games, three shots, each with under one-second on the clock, resulted in one foul, one miss and one block. That was the difference between a good season and a national championship for Virginia, bringing them redemption from an embarrassing first round loss in the previous year's tournament, the first ever by a #1 seed. Time, the first of our three major decision-making constraints, defined each of those three situations, and millions more across sports.

Being able to not only manage time but take control of it is a key decision-making advantage for playmakers. Basketball is full of time constraints, both official and unofficial. Specific official rules include the shot clock (24 seconds in the NBA/WNBA and 30 seconds in the NCAA), the five-second inbound clock, the back court clock (8 seconds in the NBA and 10 seconds in the WNBA and NCAA), the defensive three-second clock, the five-second closely guarded clock, and the ten-second free throw clock.

Those are besides four quarters or two halves, each with their own clocks counting down. Football has their play clock, which demands a sense of urgency. A penalty in hockey will give the opponent a time-based player advantage. Even sports without clocks, like baseball and golf, are considering time penalties to keep the action moving.

But, even more than some of these mandated limits, attack-oriented team sports feature one versus one battles that provide their own hurried pace. Defenders will swarm the player with the ball within seconds, but if they don't, the ball carrier will be past them. A quarterback must have an "internal clock" in his head to release the ball or run to avoid an oncoming blitzing linebacker. A point guard must trigger a pass to an open teammate under the basket before the "window of opportunity" is closed by a defender. A hockey center must hustle back on a fast break to avoid an odd man advantage overwhelming his defensemen. A batter at the plate has only four-tenths of a second to react to a 90mph fastball.

Across most sports, the time allowed to perceive, decide and act happens in seconds and, often, sub-seconds. The element of time, or lack of it, is governed by rules, manipulated with tactics and exploited with a playmaker's attention, cognition and emotions.

The Fastest OODA Wins

"The ability to operate at a faster tempo or rhythm than an adversary enables one to fold the adversary back inside himself so that he can neither appreciate nor keep up with what is going on. He will become disoriented and confused."

— JOHN BOYD

In Robert Coram's excellent biography of Air Force Colonel John Boyd, he tells a story about a conversation between Franklin "Chuck" Spinney and his mentor and hero, Boyd. It was after Iraq had invaded Kuwait in the winter of 1990. Spinney, a military analyst, brainstormed attack plans for the US Military to push Saddam Hussein's forces back into their own country. So excited with his plans, he called Boyd to reveal his strategy.

"I've thought about this a lot," said Spinney. "And there are only two options." Boyd did not respond. Spinney continued, telling Boyd of his first plan, which drew only a noncommittal grunt. Then Spinney told him of his second idea, which he thought was best: have the Marines feint an amphibious assault at Kuwait and then, with the Iraqi army's attention diverted, make a gigantic left hook far into the desert, then swing north, envelop the Iraqi Army, and annihilate them. "It's a classic single envelopment," he said. "Almost a version of the von Schlieffen Plan," a reference to the World War I invasion strategy devised by German Field Marshal Alfred von Schlieffen.

There was silence. Then Boyd said, 'Chuck, I want you to forget what you just said. You are not to discuss it with anyone else. Ever.' Boyd used a tone Spinney had never heard before. He was not issuing an order. Instead, he used a flat, no-nonsense tone that showed Spinney how deadly serious he was. Spinney was taken aback. He had been like a son to Boyd for almost fifteen years, but had never seen this side of him. Spinney stuck his plans in a box and never discussed them.[1]

The plan that Spinney described was almost exactly what Boyd was about to recommend to Dick Cheney, Secretary of the Defense under President George H. W. Bush, who had called Boyd up from an early retirement in Florida to discuss attack plans. Along with General Colin Powell, Chairman of the Joint Chiefs of Staff, Cheney was looking for better options after dismissing General Norman Schwarzkopf's "mano a mano" plan to go directly at the Iraqi Republican Guard with a traditional attrition warfare doctrine that favored slugging it out until one army falls. "I can't let Norm do this high-diddle, up the middle plan," Cheney reportedly said to Powell.

Cheney's alternative plan was directly based on Boyd's theory of warfare, which Cheney had studied back when he was a congressman from Wyoming, and the conversations they had in his SecDef office. In a bait and switch move, just as Spinney had envisioned, the Marines would fake an assault via the Persian Gulf, drawing an immediate response from what the enemy would conclude was the main thrust of the Coalition forces. Meanwhile, the Army would make a sweeping end around through the western deserts of Iraq and trap the Republican Guard from the North, pinning them against the sea. The plan worked with surprising precision. The Iraqi army was so confused that fifteen divisions of hardened fighters surrendered to just two divisions of Coalition forces. Within 100 days, they had liberated Kuwait.

Watching a press briefing on television, Spinney suddenly realized not only why his friend had been brief with him but also why Boyd had been in Washington behind closed doors with the masterminds of Desert Storm. In the briefing, Brigadier General Richard Neal explained to the world how victory over Hussein had been so swift, "We kind of got inside his decision cycle."

"Son of a bitch!" Spinney shouted. He called Boyd and said, "John, they're using your words to describe how we won the war. Everything about the war was yours. It's all right out of 'Patterns.'"[2]

"Patterns" referred to Boyd's masterpiece on military strategy, "Patterns of Conflict," his magnum opus on ground warfare throughout history, never a published book but a five hour long presentation including hundreds of

Powerpoint slides. It was a living, dynamic strategy that Boyd constantly updated with new thoughts over decades. He would present it hundreds of times, but it was the early version that Congressman Cheney heard that won Boyd an early advocate.

After Boyd's death in 1997 at age 70, Cheney would acknowledge the long-term effect that his theories held. "We could use him again now. I wish he was around now. I'd love to turn him loose on our current defense establishment and see what he could come up with. We are still oriented toward the past. We need to think about the next one hundred years rather than the last one hundred years."[3]

So, what do the military ideas of an obscure Air Force Colonel have to do with the time constraint of an athlete's decision-making? This quote from Boyd may provide the missing link.

"Every combatant observes the situation, orients himself... decides what to do and then does it. If his opponent can do this faster, however, his own actions become outdated and disconnected to the true situation, and his opponent's advantage increases geometrically. We get an image or picture in our head, which we call orientation. Then we have to make a decision as to what we're going to do and then implement the decision.... Then we look at the [resulting] action, plus our observation, and we drag in new data, new orientation, new decision, new action, ad infinitum...[4]"

Observe the situation, orient to it with a mental model,

decide on the best option then act on it. Observe, orient, decide, and act, or the OODA loop, as Boyd dubbed it. Athletes, like fighter pilots, commanders, fire fighters and any other warrior faced with a time-constrained decision, cycle through the OODA loop hundreds of times during a competition and thousands of times during a career.

But the complexity grows as each player on the field, teammates and opponents, is looping through their own OODA steps, at their own pace, based on their knowledge and experience with the game. An observation made two-seconds ago may lead to an orientation and decision that has now become obsolete as the situation develops in real-time. If he catches the error in judgement before the action occurs, a player can jump back to gain a new observation, starting the loop again.

Almost a cliche in sports, athletes and coaches talk about the game "slowing down". It's not that the actual pace of play magically changes, but that the player is processing information quicker. Put another way, their OODA loops are speeding up as their processing throughput rises.

"In a game, there are so many different variables that are thrown at you — the defense, where your teammates are, how fast your body's moving, and you have to be in control of all those decisions. So we overload in our workouts so that the game slows down in real life. It helps you become a smarter basketball player," said Steph Curry[5], point guard for the Golden State Warriors and one of the NBA's greatest playmakers of the last decade.

His long-time trainer, Brandon Payne, developed a technology-assisted workout plan to increase Curry's "neurocognitive efficiency," a marker for quicker OODA loops. "We want Stephen to take control of his defender by giving him one-two moves to see how he might be a little bit imbalanced," said Payne. "If the player is leaning left, we want to force the left foot to drop toward the basket, and we want to space backwards and to the left to give them a really odd recovery angle. It's hard to recover if your right foot is high, your left foot is low, and all of a sudden Stephen steps back to his left. A lot of times [success] will happen when he hones in on what they're trying to do."[6]

This training was just like catching the Iraqi army off-balance with an unexpected move, forcing them back to "the O's," starting their loop over. So often in sports coaching, we explain our tactics, how to react to a handful of situations and drill the playbook, assuming the game will mirror our existing mental model on how the opponent will play. Then, our opponent surprises us when, either a single player or the entire team, pulls tricks out of their bag, upsetting our preconceived plans.

Harry Hillaker, who worked with Boyd to design the F-16 fighter, agreed that the element of surprise is the key in a one versus one battle, whether it be dogfighting in the sky is supersonic jets or on the playing field.

"The key is to obscure your intentions and make them unpredictable to your opponent while you simultaneously clarify his intentions. That is, operate at a faster tempo to generate rapidly changing conditions that inhibit your opponent from adapting or reacting to those changes and that suppress or destroy his awareness. Thus, a hodgepodge of confusion and disorder occur to cause him to over or under react to conditions or activities that appear to be uncertain, ambiguous, or incomprehensible."[7]

Hillaker likes to tell the story of one of Boyd's nicknames, "40-second Boyd." After a handful of missions in the Korean War, the Air Force invited Boyd to attend the USAF Fighter Weapons School at Nellis AFB in Nevada, where he graduated top of his class. They asked him to stay on as an instructor, one of the highest achievements for any fighter pilot. He would challenge any pilot, novice or expert, to a dual in the sky with the bet that, from a position of disadvantage, he could turn the tables and "kill" his opponent in less than 40 seconds. Dozens of the best pilots tried, but no one ever beat Boyd.

"Put more succinctly, deny your opponent the use of his maneuvering advantages against you while you convert your strengths into an advantage over him and cause him to make a wrong move, one that can be easily defeated," explained Hillaker. "Time is the dominant parameter: the pilot who goes through the OODA cycle in the shortest time prevails because his opponent responds to actions that have already changed. In very simple terms, be unpredictable; operate at a pace and pattern that allows you to get him before he gets you."[8]

Given all of this background, let's walk through a sports

playmaker example of the OODA loop (see drawing below). Imagine you are a center in hockey. You just received a pass in the neutral zone (center ice) from your defenseman. There's a winger teammate on either side and slightly ahead of you. Hit the start button on your OODA loop.

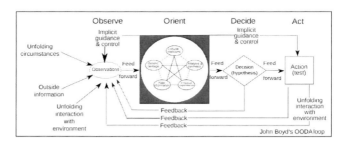

Full OODA diagram originally drawn by John Boyd

Observation

Before the puck got to your stick, you swiveled your head to take an inventory of teammates and defenders in your vicinity. Now, you turn up ice, glance left then right with your peripheral vision monitoring your flanks. The incoming sensory data is mostly visual, some say 80%, with sound filling in the details. You process the raw images of light and send the information along your optical nerve pathways to your visual cortex in a continuous stream, constantly parsed and grouped. The brain can only process information that it receives, so if an undetected defender steals the puck, there is an observation error.

Orientation

Like driving a car in traffic, the orientation step is

matching the incoming observations to your mental model. On a busy road, there are rules, patterns, even laws of physics you assume will hold true; the surrounding cars will continue in the same direction, one that is three cars behind cannot suddenly appear in front of you and a million other variables that you cannot actively track. So, we believe our mental model of how this micro world should operate, monitoring only the exceptions; a driver cuts in front of you, slams on their brakes or you get a flat tire at 60 mph. It is here that we have to re-orient ourselves to the immediate situation.

Boyd stresses that orientation sets up the decision by acclimating us to our surroundings and opportunities before our opponent. "In order to win, we should operate at a faster tempo or rhythm than our adversaries—or, better yet, get inside [the] adversary's Observation-Orientation-Decision-Action time cycle or loop ... Such activity will make us appear ambiguous (unpredictable) thereby generate confusion and disorder among our adversaries—since our adversaries will be unable to generate mental images or pictures that agree with the menacing, as well as faster transient rhythm or patterns, they are competing against."

Back to our hockey center. As soon as he received the puck, he became a target for defenders. The player covering the center immediately advances, causing a time constraint to finish the OODA loop with their next move. We see this error often with young players who panic when under pressure. The flood of sensory data is too much as they cannot orient their position and opportunities before they have to rush to a decision and act.

Playmakers can preserve the orientation step by either getting to it faster or being more efficient within it. They often have already oriented themselves before they receive the pass so they can move right to the decision. As Boyd said, "Orientation isn't just a state you're in; it's a process. You're always orienting."

Based on his traits of attention, cognition and emotions and the other constraints of tactics and rules, the center generates workable options, such as pass to a teammate, elude the oncoming defender and skate into his offensive zone or dump the puck in hoping his wingers can get to it first. The defender coming at him also has this list of standard responses in his working memory and is orienting himself at the same time. The one that can move to a decision first will often win.

Decision

Boyd always stressed that decisions are tests, not absolutes. Whether in a jet or on the ice, each choice is a data point in a repository of thousands of decisions — some work out, some don't. As this database grows, the universe of possible game changers becomes available for next time. If our young center does the same move or takes the same action every time, he becomes an easy study for future opponents. "He always goes to his right" or "he never shoots from there" or "he loses the puck under pressure" become footnotes on scouting reports, labeling the player as predictable.

As Boyd pointed out, doing the opposite is the goal of OODA: "Collapse the adversary's system into confusion and disorder causing him to over- and under-react to activity that appears simultaneously menacing as well as ambiguous, chaotic, or misleading."[9]

Act

Nothing happens without action, except maybe a turnover. If the hockey center cannot transition from decision to action, he will freeze on the spot and the defender will steal the puck. The movement option selected will depend on the player's ability to pull it off. Ego may tell him to shoot, but only his self-assessment of skill will let him know if that is a rational decision. After firing off a wild shot, memory will store that data point (along with the coach's admonition) to not try that again, at least until the center's shooting improves.

Is the OODA loop really how playmakers decide? The empirical evidence is hard to find, most likely due to the difficulty in boiling down such a fast, complicated mental process into a neat diagram. Its wide appeal among academics and practitioners spreads across multiple domains, including sports. So far, few team coaches are teaching the finer points of OODA, but we suggest it here as a helpful model for athletes.

The key takeaway is the need to process information, especially in observation and orientation, faster than the opponent. By forcing them out of their comfort zone, gained from a false security of "knowing the competition," the player across from you goes into an endless loop of observation and orientation, never arriving at a suitable decision which can delay their action long enough to beat them. Drawing from a deep inventory of skills, the playmaker can be unpredictable, avoiding labels or tendencies.

While Boyd stresses the first two steps of the loop, the actual selection of an option in the decision step is rather vague. As promised, let's revisit a framework we touched on in our first book, recognition-primed decisions, that dives deeper into real world research on how the playmaker pulls the trigger on an action.

The Midfield Maestro

In the traditional France Football interview with the winner of the annual Ballon D'Or award, given to the best soccer player in the world, Luka Modrić recalled a conversation he had with Zinedine Zidane, his Real Madrid manager, two years prior.

"When I recounted all of the individual trophies that I've won this year and when I saw that I was among the 30 [Ballon D'Or] finalists, I began to believe it, but there's one thing I'll never forget. When Zidane became Madrid coach in January 2016, he called me to his office one day after training and told me how he saw me as a player and what he expected of me. He told me that I was an important player for him and, above all, that he saw me as a player who could win the Ballon d'Or."

"When someone like Zidane, with all of his personality and history, tells you that, it boosts your confidence. I admired him and respected him enormously as a player, he saw me as someone like himself, quiet and a bit shy, he expected me to express myself more on the pitch, to open up. He needed me to be a key part of the team in an era when we were truly playing well. Those words from Zidane helped me to go further in my play. Even in spite of his words, I didn't begin to believe it."[10]

By winning the 2018 award, he became the first player in a decade not named Messi or Ronaldo to take home the trophy. It highlighted a spectacular year for Modrić, who had already become a midfield mainstay in a star-studded Real Madrid line-up.

Starting in December 2017, the Los Blancos won their third consecutive FIFA Club World Cup with Modrić being named the best player of the competition. In the spring of 2018, the club won its third consecutive Champions League, where Modrić won the best midfielder award being named to the tournament's best XI.

Then there was the 2018 World Cup in Russia, where a talented but underrated Croatian team fought their way to the Final against France. Despite losing 4-2, Modrić was the tournament's best overall player, bringing home the Golden Ball trophy. Finally, he collected year-end awards for FIFA Men's Player of the Year and the IFFHS World's Best Playmaker award. As a bonus, Modrić's number 10 Real Madrid jersey became the club's bestseller after the departure of Cristiano Ronaldo. And in 2019, Modrić won the Golden Foot award, given to players at least 28 years old, still playing and "who stand out for their athletic achievements (both as individuals and team players) and for their personality[11]."

Zidane, who was also a former Real Madrid midfield legend and 1998 Ballon D'Or winner, knows exactly why Modrić is special. "It's his tranquility," said Zidane. "It's his tranquility with the ball. I have the best players and we could talk about any of them, but if you ask me about Luka, I have to talk about his calmness with the ball at his feet. La tranquilidad. That's what he gives to the team when he's playing well. He makes the rest play."[12]

Gareth Bale, a teammate of Modrić in their early days at Tottenham in the English Premier League and now at Real Madrid, adds vision as a differentiator. "He just always seems to be consistent, and he sees passes no one else sees," said Bale. "Being with him at Tottenham and at Real Madrid, I've been able to witness it many times." Other world class managers agree with Modrić's nickname, "the Midfield Maestro," including Jose Mourinho, Sir Alex Ferguson and Carlo Ancelotti who confirmed, "I can only tell you Luka Modrić is definitely one of best midfield players in the world."[13]

At 5' 7" tall and a slight 143 pounds, Modrić is a wispy flash of motion on the field with his long, sandy brown hair parted in the middle and pinned to his head with a black rubber-band headband. Never scoring over three goals or seven assists in any of his eight years at Real Madrid (or at Tottenham except for one season scoring four goals), casual fans wonder how he commands so much respect. As a deep-lying midfielder, Modrić is the team quarterback, to borrow from another sport, setting up plays by creating time for his teammates to get open. Watching game after game, you will see tiny moves, side-stepping opponents as they lunge at him while keeping his eyes downfield, searching for the next best option.

Digging deeper into soccer statistics shows this next level of playmaking. Completing his 13th professional season in 2020 at 34, Modrić continues to be in the top ten of several playmaker stat categories for La Liga, considered one of the three best leagues in the world: assists per 90 minutes - 5th, passes into the opponent's third of the field - 6th, goal-creating actions per 90 minutes - 3rd, points per match - 5th, +/- per 90 minutes (team goals scored - team goals against) - 5th.

Even with the hindsight of analytics (which we'll cover in a later chapter), the work rate, positioning and, as Zidane noted, the tranquility that Modrić brings to the field has to be seen to be appreciated. Certainly, those that know the game understand his contributions as a playmaker. Modrić was once again named to the 2019 FIFPro World 11 for the fifth consecutive year, as voted by over 45,000 professional soccer players around the world.

"There's a saying that the best things in life don't come easily and I believe that," Modrić added in his France Football interview. "My life has been based on fighting and on achieving objectives through hard work. It hasn't been easy, but I have won it. History will say that a Croatian player, representing his small country, won the Ballon d'Or after Cristiano Ronaldo and Lionel Messi, who are players at another level. Nobody has the right to compare themselves to them. They are the best in the history of this sport. To come after them is incredible, although I don't think for one second that it's over for them. I consider myself a normal person and act that way, while I see that people see me as such. They see me as a humble person. I am happy that someone normal is able to win the Ballon d'Or."[14]

Forced to flee with his family at age six to the port city of Zadar after a group of Serbian Chetniks brutally murdered his beloved grandfather then burned down their house as the family escaped, Modrić endured a childhood trying to insert soccer into a violent environment. Living in a hotel and playing in a parking lot filled with grenade craters, the young Modrić attracted attention even in the most surreal surroundings. Coaches from the local club, NK

Zadar, came to watch him and soon signed him to their academy.

"His touch was soft, velvety and precise. For a novice [seven-year-old] it was amazing,"[15] said Davorin Matosevic, one of Modrić's first coaches at Zadar. Air-raid sirens and mortar fire regularly chased the kids into shelters during practice, but Modrić was unfazed by the war or the evaluations that labeled him talented but undersized.

"For me it was evident that he was destined to become a great," said Miodrag Paunovic, another Zadar youth coach. "He was a ballplayer. However, not many believed in him because he was so thin and looked as delicate as a leaf. At that time in the Balkans, the key idea was that you had to be powerful to be a success in football."

Maturing a bit physically in his early teens, scouts noticed his play for the country's biggest club, Dinamo Zagreb and the Croatian under-15 national team. After impressive spells in Bosnia with a rough adult league and more seasoning back in Croatia, the big clubs came calling, including Arsenal, Manchester United and Barcelona. But it was Tottenham who ultimately signed him, igniting a 17 year career to the top of the soccer world.

"My grandfather was killed, and I have been through a lot of things in my childhood but when you go through what I went through as a kid, it helps you put things in perspective and you don't stress yourself all the time," said Modrić. "You accept that every defeat, or every obstacle, is part of football and you learn to live with it. All the things that happened in my childhood helped me to become more tough, to believe in myself and to fight for my dreams. I never gave up and every doubt for me was extra motivation to prove people wrong or prove I can do something. When I was doing something I did well, it gave me even more confidence or strength for the next challenge. That was important for me not to give up."

Modrić's advice to the next generation is to believe. "I say that to young kids: never stop believing in yourself, not even when people tell you that you cannot do this. It is the only way you can succeed in something, not just in sport, but in general. You have to believe in yourself, taking motivation from things people are saying. That helped me never to give up. I am a fighter in general and it never crossed my mind to give up because someone said something."[16]

So, what makes Luka Modrić so extraordinary at exploiting time as he makes decisions? Positioned in the middle of a soccer field with teammates constantly on the move and defenders coming at him from all angles, how does the Maestro speed up his OODA loop, especially the decision step? To explore this fundamental skill, we asked an intellectual giant in the field who has pursued the same questions in many other pressure-packed environments besides sports.

"I didn't see anybody comparable to him, even on France's team. Modrić, he was the guy who was orchestrating it all," said Dr. Gary Klein, recalling the 2018

World Cup during an interview with us. "He was the playmaker, he really was. He was an exemplar in his team, punched way above his weight. So, definitely the recognition-primed decision (RPD) process was being used there. It's about how can people make decisions, rapid decisions under uncertainty, because you're dealing with an adversary who is trying to be deceptive as well. How can a team make those kinds of decisions without looking at all the options, because there's not time to do it? That's what the RPD model is all about."[17]

Seeing What Other's Don't

Gary Klein did not follow the typical academic route. After graduating from the University of Pittsburgh with a Ph.D. in experimental psychology, he spent four years as an assistant professor at Oakland University before moving on to research for the US Air Force. In 1978, he founded his first private research firm, preferring to study people in their natural, decision-making habitat rather than in sterile, variable-controlled lab experiments.

Specifically, he focused on decisions under a time constraint when the stakes are high, such as those made by military and medical personnel and first-responders where choices need to happen quickly but carefully as the consequences of a poor decision can be deadly. While the in-game decisions of athletes are never at the same risk level of these other domains, the outcomes mean something within the world of sports.

"Instead of beginning with formal models of decision-making, we began by conducting field research to try to discover the strategies people used," Klein explained. "Instead of looking for ways that people were suboptimal, we wanted to find out how people were able to make tough decisions under difficult conditions such as limited time, uncertainty, high stakes, vague goals, and unstable conditions."[18]

Let's set-up a sports scenario, going back to our expert, Luka Modrić. In their second group game of World Cup 2018, Croatia faced Lionel Messi's Argentina, a top-five favorite to win the tournament. In their first game, Croatia had beaten Nigeria while Argentina had surprisingly tied with Iceland. With a win, Croatia would go through to the Round of 16 at the top of the group. In the 53rd minute, Willy Caballero, Argentina's keeper, flubbed a pass to his defender, letting Ante Rebic volley the wayward ball into the net for a 1-0 Croatia lead. Despite Argentina controlling 58% of the possession, Modrić broke the game open in the 80th minute.

On a counterattack after an intercepted pass at midfield, four Croatian players raced upfield with the ball against five Argentinian defenders. A sixth defender arrived as Modrić received the ball in the center of the field, about 25 yards from the goal.

Right before the ball arrived, Modrić flashed a look behind to see that the only defender nearby was the one standing in front of him about two yards away. Mario Mandzukic, the Croatian forward, was standing at the top of the 18-yard box with Gabriel Mercado covering him. Modrić's other two teammates were to his left, somewhat open but with four more defenders spaced evenly in a line protecting the box.

Instantly, Modrić faked a shot to the right, causing center back Nicolas Otamendi to stick out his left leg to block it. Modrić shifted his weight to the left with Otamendi trying to recover, then the Croatian took the ball two steps back to his right, lining up Mandzukic and Mercado between himself and Caballero. With Otamendi a step behind, Modrić unleashed a right-footed rocket that curled around the player screen he had just created, the ball soaring into the net just inside the right post.

Four seconds had elapsed from the time Modrić received the ball to its release from his deadly right boot. The decision to shoot from 25 yards away in a one goal game in the World Cup took two seconds. A bold choice that deflated Argentina, who ended up losing the game by three goals after another blunder in front of Caballero in stoppage time.

Using Klein's RPD as a decision-making framework, let's break down this sequence to understand Modrić's thought process (although we'll never know, as he did not discuss the goal in his post-game comments). A good place to start is asking what exactly is the definition of a decision?

"This is an important question because the academic field of decision-making identifies a decision as choosing between options," Dr. Klein told us. "In fact, what we found is people do not choose between options. They adopt a course of action when options are available, but they may not consider all of them. That was one of the unique discoveries that was important for coming up with the RPD model is it was a decision point. They were plausible options, and people were able to adopt a course of action in that circumstance."[19]

For important decisions that lack a sense of urgency measured in seconds, like buying a car or getting a loan, we can default to a more familiar stepwise procedure that includes naming the desired outcome, researching options, filtering and ranking those options, then applying a logic-based process to select the best choice. All of this is possible with the luxury of time.

But in his research interviews with captains of fire departments, soldiers and police officers, Dr. Klein discovered that they often only generated only one option for a critical situation, then took action. Or at least they only remembered coming up with one option, which to their experienced mind seemed an obvious and natural reaction.

According to RPD, when time is of the essence, the expert must go straight to the top of the list and mentally simulate that option. If it works out in his head, in less than a second, then he "goes with his gut" even though that gut decision is based on years of cataloguing similar patterns in his brain. This specific situation may not exactly match any of the previous experiences logged in his memory, but the brain can generalize enough to find a best match.

Klein calls this process "satisficing," a combination of satisfy and suffice. There's no time to cycle through all the options, so if the first one works in a quick mind experiment, then it is chosen and executed. This is how the Decision and Act steps of the OODA loop get sped up, and why the Orientation step is critical to activate the subconscious mind to find a solution.

"The focus is on the way they assess the situation and judge it familiar, not on comparing options," said Klein. "Courses of action can be quickly evaluated by imagining how they will be carried out, not by formal analysis and comparison. The emphasis is on being poised to act rather than being paralyzed until all the evaluations have been completed.[20]"

For Modrić, long-range shooting is not only familiar but a strength. In his eight seasons with Real Madrid, he has scored 15 of his 21 goals (over 70%) from beyond the 18-yard box, with a few as deep as 25 yards away.[21] To put the relative distance in perspective, that's like basketball's Curry burying shots from a few steps behind the three-point line, or Zdeno Chara, the Boston Bruins' massive, veteran defenseman, ripping a 100 mph slapshot from outside the blue line. Because Modrić knew he had the skill from experience, the decision to shoot rather than pass to a teammate was the first "workable" option, as Klein defines it in his book, Sources of Power[22]:

"Decision makers usually look for the first workable option they can find, not the best option. Since the first option they consider is usually workable, they do not have to generate a large set of options to be sure they get a good one. They generate and evaluate options one at a time and do not bother comparing the advantages and disadvantages of alternatives. By imagining the option being carried out, they can spot weaknesses and find ways to avoid these, thereby making the option stronger. Conventional models just select the best, without seeing how it can be improved."[23]

In this specific scenario versus Argentina, Modrić experienced what Klein calls "variation 1", out of three, of the RPD process. Even before Modrić received the ball, he sensed his surroundings by looking over his shoulders. At one point, he stretched his arms out wide to his teammate to signal that he was wide open for a pass. The pattern he recognized was one that had been successful for him in the past; receive the ball just outside the 18-yard box with no immediate defender.

As the RPD model states, the scene was typical and familiar and has four byproducts; there are relevant cues present, the plausible goals remain the same, there are expectancies of what will happen next and a course of action is apparent. Since Modrić's memory contained so many similar sequences from the hundreds of games he has played, he could proceed with the option to shoot, even if from far away, because the game primed his recognition.

In variation 2, the orientation to the situation does not match up so nicely with memory. Maybe if Otamendi had been much closer to Modrić when he received the ball, the time to respond would have disappeared, forcing Modrić to reassess. Or perhaps Otamendi and another defender might have immediately closed in on Modrić after he had the ball, breaking his expectancies of what he could do next.

Variation 3 happens when the diagnosis of the situation is familiar, triggering a recognition from memory, but the decision-maker feels the first action option, usually linked to the situation, will not work. In that case, Modrić may have recognized a typical scenario, but when he instantly simulated the shot in his mind, he sensed a problem causing him to back out before he sent the command to his body to shoot.

"One way to think about these three variations is that variation 1 is basically an 'if... then' reaction, an antecedent followed by the rule-based response," explains Klein. "The expertise is in being able to recognize when the antecedent condition has been met. Variation 2 take the form 'if (?) . . .then', with the decision maker deliberating about the nature of the situation. Variation 3 takes the form 'if. . . then (?)' as the decision maker ponders the outcome of a reaction."[24]

The challenge with every time-constrained decision is

the fear of failure or, at a minimum, making a mistake. If Modrić's shot does not curl inside the post, the reaction from teammates, coaches and fans may be that he was selfish, passing up other possibly better options. As we discussed in our chapter on emotions, self-confidence reigns supreme with consistent, accurate decisions. With mistakes comes self-doubt, causing either RPD variation 2 or 3, extending the OODA loop and giving the opponent more time to react. That is why freedom to make decisions, experience mistakes and catalog them as experiences is critical to young playmakers.

The opportunity to build their tacit knowledge, (intellect that cannot be easily explained), helps novices grow into experts. Coaches should encourage kids to think on their own during scrimmages and practices so they have creative intuition during games.

Dr. Klein explains, "I think it's too bad when the training in youth sports is about not making mistakes. It is very procedural. It's getting these drills down. Part of the assumption is once you get all the basics down, at some point later on in your career, you can learn about the decision-making part, but now you have all kinds of negative transfer to overcome that you have to overcome the way you've been taught to do it."

"The decision-making should be there from the very start. That's the way of building adaptive models, rather than trying to graft it on later. Kids become paralyzed because they are afraid of making mistakes. You see the tension. You see how nervous they are that they'll be blamed if they don't execute the way that they were taught.[25]"

The opposite of a mistake reduction strategy is to encourage and grow intuition and innovation. As we will discuss later, tactics from a coach need to be a framework of play, not a drilled instruction set. When the tactics are too rigid, a player will freeze when they encounter a situation that has not appeared in training. They cannot generalize the pattern and plan a response quickly.

"Intuition depends on the use of experience to recognize key patterns that indicate the dynamics of the situation. Because patterns can be subtle, people often cannot describe what they noticed, or how they judged a situation as typical or atypical. Therefore, intuition has a strange reputation. Skilled decision makers know that they can depend on their intuition, but at the same time they may feel uncomfortable trusting a source of power that seems so accidental."[26]

There is no shortcut to the fast cognitive reactions of a playmaker. Getting inside an opponent's OODA loop by drawing on a trained memory of thousands of situations, actions and outcomes requires this sixth sense of knowing the right thing to do at the right time. Nothing builds this faster than exposure to hours of fun, competitive play where mistakes happen, to be indexed and remembered without the harsh reprimands that kill creativity. Modrić grew up in a stressful environment, but not on the soccer field.

"The nature of expertise depends so heavily on tacit knowledge, and that is very hard to unpack," reminds Klein.

"It involves recognizing patterns, making perceptual discriminations, building stronger mental models, shifting mindsets. None of these things are easily elicited. That's why it's tacit or passive knowledge. It's not really possible to articulate and encode everything that an expert or much of what an expert knows and then teach it in a way that's meaningful. That seems to be a dead end."[27]

5

RULES

"Serious sport has nothing to do with fair play. It is bound up with hatred, jealousy, boastfulness, disregard of all rules and sadistic pleasure in witnessing violence. In other words, it is war minus the shooting."

— GEORGE ORWELL

I n week 3 of the 2019 NFL season, the nationally televised Thursday Night Football game featured the Tennessee Titans and the Jacksonville Jaguars. Not exactly a ratings bonanza matchup, but it was too early in the season for Fox Sports to flex to a more intriguing game. Still, NFL players who are sitting at home waiting for their Sunday kickoff will watch whatever is on just because its professional football. By the second quarter, one viewer in particular couldn't take it anymore.

"Too many penalties. Just let us play!!! #TENvsJac" was his first tweet.[1] Less than ten minutes later, he followed up with, "I'm turning off this game. I can't watch these ridiculous penalties anymore #TENvsJAC".[2] Now, some would say that Tom Brady, probably the greatest quarterback ever to play in the NFL, was proactively lobbying for fewer offensive penalties called on his New England Patriots three days later. But, when a six-time Super Bowl champion makes a public complaint on the state of officiating in his league, things happen quickly.

In just the first half of that game, the officiating crew called an eye-popping eight offensive holding penalties. That compares to an average of only 2.8 holding calls per game throughout the 2018 season. In fact, in the first two weeks of last season, plus that Thursday Night game, (a total of 33 games), the league averaged 5.7 offensive holding calls per game. That raised the per game average for all penalties to 7.9, the highest rate since stats were first tracked in 1941.

Two days later, Al Riveron, VP of NFL officiating, held a Saturday conference call with league officials, presumably to discuss current events. Lo-and-behold, 24 hours later, the Sunday games averaged 2.9 offensive holding calls, right back in line with rates of the recent past.

Going into the season, the NFL Competition Committee had added offensive holding to its list of "points of emphasis," specifically stating, "offensive holding will be more strictly enforced this season, particularly on the back side of the run play or line of scrimmage. Referees will closely monitor play at the line of scrimmage to ensure that offensive players do not materially restrict opponents or alter the defender's path or angle of pursuit."[3]

As Mike Pereira, who previously held Riveron's position, explained to football fans, "Basically what [Riveron] said to them was 'You're doing a good job based on what the competition committee wanted you to do: call holding on the backside of the play. But let's not overreact.'"[4] It's one thing to agree in a conference room to a set of proposed rule changes, but something quite different when the league's best player voices his disapproval publicly.

Even with team by team meetings and video examples of rule infractions, football players, even at the professional level, are creatures of habit, using techniques learned over years of practices, drills and games. Besides the eagle-eyed officials, the linemen's slow change to the new rule interpretation resulted in a flurry of flags.

At the start of the 2018 season, the same cycle of emphasis followed by enforcement occurred when the "roughing the quarterback" penalty seemed to be a focal point for officials as there were 9.6 such flags per week in the first five weeks. But then, after two nationally televised and controversial calls against Green Bay Packers linebacker Clay Matthews, that number dropped to 5.5 per week for the rest of the season. Again, it may have been a combination of the players adapting plus the higher standard being relaxed a bit when it was apparent that the game would suffer.

The World Needs Rules

Rules are necessary in life and in sport. Without them, organized sport would not exist. In fact, each sport is defined by its rules. How long does the game last? What is the size of the playing surface? How does a team score? What do the laws of the game allow and forbid? When making any of hundreds of decisions during a game, an athlete applies the expansive filter of rules prior to every potential action. "I can do this but not that." "I can't do that but I may do it anyway." "I knew that I couldn't do that but, at the moment, I forgot and made a mistake." Some are conscious, albeit instant, decisions to break the rule, hoping not to get caught. Some infractions are subconscious, arising from a lack of attention.

As we have discussed, the demands of perception, cognition and emotions overfill the working memory, leaving little room to juggle the constraints of time, tactics and rules.

Arguing with a referee's call after the fact has become an obsession with many fans and almost a tactic for players and coaches trying to affect the psyche of an official. Penalties, fouls, and rule violations define a game, able to swing momentum and, possibly, the outcome. Written in complex rule books, the language describing each infraction is up for interpretation in a split second, then disputed by the guilty side. The new frontier of video review replay is helping to "get the call right" post hoc, even when no call was initially made, but is changing the game at a fundamental level of flow and momentum. As the list of rules that can be challenged with video review increases, players will realize the odds of surreptitiously cheating will fall.

How complicated are each sport's rules? One way to judge the complexity is by sheer volume; throw the rule books down a stairwell and see which one makes the loudest thud. In a more elegant method, Dan Kozikowski, a sports fan and professional data wonk, took it on himself to count the words in each official rule book for the most popular sports as a complexity metric.[5]

American football won easily, with the National Football League (NFL) rule book clocking in at 68,479 words. The National Hockey League's (NHL) tome came in at 58,584 and Major League Baseball (MLB) followed at 48,657 words. The National Basketball Association (NBA) rule book comprised a reasonable 37,812 words with FIFA soccer totaling a mere 23,156 words.

Does complexity in rules equal more interruptions during a game because of more opportunities for player mistakes? There is a correlation, as Kirk Goldsberry and Katherine Rowe at FiveThirtyEight Sports detailed early in

2020. As they watched Super Bowl LIV, the paltry minutes of actual game action surprised and irked them. They wondered, "what, exactly, are we all watching?"[6]

As part of a sports analytics course they taught at the University of Texas, they clocked the entire timeline of dozens of games in the major sports, categorizing each minute in three buckets, game action, non-action and commercials. Game action is live player movement while non-action includes game stoppages, such as time-outs, out-of-bounds sequences, and penalty calls. And then there are the commercials... so many commercials.

They found that NFL games that lasted over three hours in total duration comprised just 18 total minutes of on-field action, 140 minutes of non-action and 50 minutes of commercials (which are obviously non-action on the field but they counted them as additional minutes). MLB games were not much better, showing only 23 minutes of game action within an average game length of 3 hours, 45 minutes. The NHL rulebook is daunting, but in games that averaged two-and-a-half hours, the researchers counted roughly 63 minutes of puck movement (including overtime), about the same as non-action time. That makes sense for sports with game clocks that stop, but there is much less time spent during those stoppages.

The sports with the shortest rule books, basketball and soccer, delivered plenty of action. NBA games analyzed by Goldsberry and Rowe showed 50 minutes of action (some with overtime) compared to 62 minutes of non-action. By far the best bang for a sports fan's efficiency buck is soccer, specifically English Premier League, which showed nearly 60 minutes of play across a two-hour game. The running clock in soccer steals from the 90-minute total with stoppages, substitutions, etc, but the referee, theoretically, adds those minutes back at the end of the game.

Still, the simplicity of soccer rules contributes to the flow of the game, allowing players to focus more on the other constraints of decision-making, time (before a defender arrives) and tactics. Fouls, offsides and handballs are the three primary rules for a player to consider, freeing processing capacity in the brain for more creative tasks.

But American football's laundry list of possible infractions, including movement, formations, physical dos and don'ts, before and after the snap, and even celebrations can overwhelm a player's working memory. Across the 256 total NFL games in 2019, officials called 3,572 penalties for an average of 14 per game. There is an assumption that players know the rules and understand how breaking the rules can hurt their team's chances of winning. If not, coaches remind them in no uncertain terms at Monday film sessions by their coaching staff.

So why, at the highest level of sport, do these rule violations happen? Why were there an average of twenty personal fouls called per game in the NBA over the last decade?[7] Why do NHL teams average just over eight minutes of penalties per game?[8] Even in the beautiful game, why do English Premier League teams average eleven fouls, two offsides and two yellow cards per game?[9] Just telling players to stop making those poor decisions is not working. So, let's dive deeper into not only why players break the rules but what happens when they either lose focus or choose unwisely.

Rules Were Made To Be Broken

We touched on this earlier but now it is time to break down the rule universe. As defined by the Oxford English dictionary, "one of a set of explicit or understood regulations or principles governing conduct within a particular activity or sphere."[10] In sports, we have rules to keep the game fair. Again from Oxford, fair is "in accordance with the rules or standards."[11] Because a sport, "an activity involving physical exertion and skill in which an individual or team competes against another or others for entertainment[12]," is less interesting or even unplayable if players succumb to their "hatred, jealousy, boastfulness, disregard of all rules and sadistic pleasure," as Orwell claims.

How many church softball games have ended in brawls because of a disagreement over rules or the lack of an umpire to enforce them? The desire to win the game clouds our usually high moral judgment and sense of fairness. Teams scheme to find wrinkles or inconsistencies or vagueness in the stated rules to exploit to gain an advantage. Opponents complain to the official about these egregious violations only to have the cunning coach explain that he did nothing wrong… according to the rules.

After all, as the saying goes, rules are meant to be broken. The irony is that these creative loopholes may work for the current season, only to have the sport's governing body discuss, debate and, in most cases, define the rule more clearly or add an entirely new one to the rule book.

The NFL, creator of the heavyweight champion rule book, cites this logic in a feature on the evolution of rules on their website:

"Imagine the NFL if the rules of play had never changed: A quarterback can't throw a pass unless he's at least 5 yards behind the line of scrimmage. The offense begins some plays just a yard from the sideline and is penalized for throwing more than one pass during a series of downs. Player substitutions are prohibited. No communication from the sideline is allowed. Players from both teams grab their opponents' facemasks at will."

"Of course, that's not how professional football is played today. Throughout the history of the NFL, the custodians of the game not only have protected its integrity but also have revised its playing rules to make the contests fairer, safer and more entertaining.[13]"

They then explain why the kickoff line has been moved three times between 1974 and 2011. First, in 1974, from the 40 to the 35 to "rev up the game, the change was made to produce more exciting returns." When these returns lagged again in mid-90s, the line was moved back even more to the 30-yard-line.

But in 2011, because of returns that were so full of energy that they caused injuries, the NFL put the kickoff line back at the 35, eliminated running starts by the kicking team and disallowed wedge blocks by the receiving team. Concussions suffered on kickoffs did drop by 40 percent, which was the goal of the changes, mostly because the return rate dropped from 80 percent to almost 50 percent.

More confusing for athletes, young and old, is when rules change at a skill level that requires adjustments to style and technique learned over years of practice. Just ask Clay Matthews, linebacker for the Los Angeles Rams. As we alluded to earlier, starting in 2018 when he was with the Packers, the league made the "roughing the passer" penalty a point of emphasis with more restrictions on how and where a defender could tackle a passer who most of the time was the quarterback.

Early in the season, for three weeks in a row, different referees flagged Matthews for the penalty after he sacked the quarterback of three different teams. But video replays seemed to show that Matthews was staying within the somewhat gray areas of the rule, with media, players and analysts befuddled on what exactly he did wrong.

"I thought Clay did exactly what he's supposed to do there," said Mike McCarthy, head coach of the Packers. "He hit him with his shoulder, he was coming full speed off of a block, he braced himself, so I was fine with what Clay did." Even Dean Blandino, former head of NFL officials and now a TV analyst, sounded confused, "I just don't know what more he's supposed to do," he said. "I don't like that as a foul."[14]

Matthews, in his defense, said he understands the emphasis that the league was after, to protect vulnerable and valuable quarterbacks. But, after playing football for over ten years, the requirement to become more passive and less aggressive takes time to relearn both technically and emotionally. "I understand the spirit of the rule, I said it weeks prior," said Matthews. "But when you have a hit like that, that's a football play. I even went up to [quarterback] Alex Smith after the game, asked him, 'What do you think? What can I do differently? Because that's a football play.' I hit him from the front, got my head across, wrapped up. I've never heard of anybody tackling somebody without any hands. If I wanted to hurt him, I could have. I could've put some extra on him. That's football."[15]

Whether the call is roughing the passer, pass interference, or holding in football or personal fouls in basketball or interference in hockey, these tweaks to the rules disrupt a player's ingrained automaticity, that subconscious skill that requires no active thinking.

As we learned with Kahneman's System 1 and System 2, an athlete learns to decide slowly, using System 2 learning through years of trial and error. Hopefully, those decisions become automatic responses transferred into System 1 reactions.

For players like Matthews, their learned task was to escape from their blocker, sprint to the quarterback and tackle him, all in less than three seconds before he releases a pass. He knew the old rule of what could and could not be done and had overlaid that information into his attack plan. Then, the rules changed, literally, and he has to adjust on the fly breaking the practiced patterns, monitoring his timing, angle and acceleration to meet the freshly minted and mandated guidelines of the league.

For the record, Section 2, Article 11 of the NFL Rule Book defining the roughing the passer personal foul requires 1,033 words, roughly three pages of text detailing the finer points of legally tackling a quarterback.[16] For Matthews and the referees, the learning journey continues. In week 5 of the 2019 season, the Seattle Seahawks were trailing with under six minutes in the game.

Quarterback Russell Wilson threw an incomplete pass on first down but the referee called a roughing the passer call on Matthews as he tackled Wilson just after he released the ball. Replays show that Matthews used his shoulder to hit Wilson in the shoulder, a clean hit as defined by the rule. Nevertheless, the 15-yard penalty was enforced, the Seahawks drive continued, and they later scored the winning touchdown. It seemed Matthews had learned the new rule and adjusted his "how to tackle the quarterback" program in his brain. Perhaps it was the referee who still needed to update the code in his head to reflect the new definition.

The Other Side of the Whistle

While the subject of rules and compliance is constantly on the minds of athletes, coaches, fans and media, there has been surprisingly little research on how players learn, internalize and process the framework of rules when playing the game. If you played sports growing up, take a minute to think about how you learned your favorite game including its structure, strategy and, of course, the rules.

Like most budding playmakers, you probably watched your heroes on TV - slowly, implicitly learning the ins and outs of what everyone was doing. Through observation and listening to not only the announcers but also your family and friends commenting on the game, the patchwork fabric of how the game works seeped into your subconscious.

Next, you met your friends on the playground at school, mimicking a home run swing or a long pass to your classmate you had seen on TV the night before. There were playground rules that bore some resemblance to the pros, but they had their own quirks; the street light was the left field foul pole, the two oak tree trunks were the goalposts, it was two-hand touch until the teacher wasn't looking then it was full tackle.

In that specific environment, your brain logged the special condition rules, and you did your best to abide by them. But arguments broke out. There was always the one kid who needed to get his way when he struck out or fumbled the ball. The rules, according to him, were very clear that a foul tip which nobody heard, was not the third strike. Or that his knee was already on the ground before he fumbled. Words were exchanged, some pushing and shoving, then it was back to the game with a more clearly defined rule modification ("OK, from now on, your little brother doesn't get four strikes.")

Then, we graduated into organized sport, with uniforms, coaches, parents and, heaven forbid, real referees, umpires, and linesmen. There was one set of rules that the striped-shirt official administered and everyone had to follow.

These brave souls were, at different times during a single game, loved, reviled, cheered, booed, and questioned about their eyesight or sanity. Just like the athletes they watched over, these men and women sprinted, sidestepped, and spun while trying to keep their direct focus on the action while monitoring the remaining players with their peripheral vision. And just as players had to constantly perceive, decide and execute, officials also required fast and accurate decision-making skills. Players and coaches dread the sound of the whistle signaling an upcoming rule infraction.

But officials deal with their own stress and anxiety from having to correctly interpret thousand-word foul descriptions in the blink of an eye while managing the emotions of players, coaches and fans, at least half of whom won't like each call made.

All of this fervent attention given to officials and their calls has led to a much larger database of studies, frameworks and theories regarding their responsibilities. To enlighten the athlete's learning process, let's take a detour to understand the decision-making process of officials. By understanding their process, we might borrow what we learned to apply to players.

Managing the Game

Playing for the Bronze Medal in any tournament is an underperforming rarity for any USA Basketball Men's National Team. But to play it against the host country in their stadium made it particularly unusual. That was the scene in early August 1998 at the Athens Olympic Indoor Hall as the Greeks played the Americans. Upset that their home team had lost their bid for the championship in overtime to Yugoslavia the day before and now playing a team from the States that featured no NBA players, the Greek fans were hungry for any medal on their soil.

To their credit, the USA team, comprising players who played overseas and a few college players thanks to that year's NBA lockout, had taken Russia to the limit, only losing by two points in their semi-final game.

Bill Mildenhall, an Australian Hall of Fame referee who later officiated the Barcelona and Sydney Olympic Games, was part of the crew that night. Down by 20 points, with only a few minutes left in the game, the Greek supporters grew restless with their hopes for an international basketball podium all but gone. The star of the Greek team and their leading scorer was apparently fouled on a three point attempt, or at least his display of falling abruptly to the floor convinced the home crowd that he had been assaulted. As Mildenhall recalled in a 2012 article, the Greek player acted, "as though he had been hit by a cannon."[17]

The Greek fans immediately erupted. Assessing the situation, the score, and the time left on the clock, Mildenhall whistled the American player for a foul, while knowing none had been committed. The USA player approached him incredulously, surprised that the obvious flop had fooled the experienced referee. Mildenhall quietly agreed that there was no foul but confided to the American, "looking around at the current situation, what was my best avenue?" Appreciative of his candor, the American nodded and let the game finish with no further incident.

This is the tricky balancing act of making decisions as a referee or any official in sport; strict adherence to the rules versus putting them in the moment's context, better known as game management. As with athlete decision-making, the information immediately available determines the quality of choices. Officials often face knowledge gaps, both before and during the game.

In the article where he retold the Greece-USA moment, Mildenhall and Dr. Clare MacMahon, senior lecturer of exercise science at La Trobe University and an expert in the psychology of officiating, addressed the nuances of game management or "calibration" within the duties of a referee being an objective arbiter of the rules.

"In this sense, game management can be considered to be the result of officials choosing to fill knowledge gaps with information from the context of the game. While officials may not base decision-making on game management, there is certainly a great deal of support for the position that good officials are mindful of the current situation and make adjustments in their decision-making processes to accommodate it. Game context provides more information in an information-poor task and is regularly referred to as reading and understanding the game."[18]

Not only do referees use context information from previous games but also set a tone for how to officiate compared to other sports, especially for a high-profile event watched by millions around the world. Mildenhall recalled the instructions received prior to another world championship tournament:

"The pre-tournament meetings for the 2010 Basketball World Championships emphasized that the most significant feature of officiating would need to be managing games so that all games were officiated fairly and all teams would come away happy with the result, with no ensuing controversies. The meeting noted the officiating issues experienced at the 2010 FIFA World Cup, and how important it was for FIBA not to have any similar controversies.

The referees were expected to maintain complete control and therefore were encouraged to use all their management skills to ensure the correct team won the game, with the losing team still willing to shake hands and thank the game officials after the game. This philosophy to officiating the tournament seems to have been successful; given that the report from all games was that the officiating was not an issue. Even potentially volatile countries were complimentary about the officiating even when they had been defeated, sometimes by very small margins. This illustrates that, particularly at the elite level, using game management and context is considered a method of managing information gaps and is a skill."[19]

Studied examples from different sports highlight this attempt to keep the game competitive. While not calling phantom fouls, officials have shown tendencies to balance the whistles out. In a soccer study,[20] researchers found that referees were more likely to award a penalty if they had not called one previously in a close call. They were less likely to call consecutive penalties against the same team.

Considered by the researchers as evidence of bias, other observers labeled it good game management by those referees. In a 2009 study of NCAA college basketball decisions, researchers found a statistical pattern of calling more fouls against the team with either fewer total fouls, the team winning or the visiting team.[21]

Another way to look at game management is the use of heuristics, or rules of thumb, by the referee. Much like a player's automaticity in sport skills, a referee builds a knowledge base of what is possible for the level of athlete she is observing. Again, to fill in missing pieces of information, a referee may subconsciously apply heuristics to judge if an action taken by a player is possible.

"For example, if asked to judge whether a player is offside, not having viewed the player's entire movements, a football referee may use the availability heuristic, to search her memory for any experience of a player at that level of play moving with such speed from an onside position," write MacMahon and Mildenhall. "This is then factored in to how plausible it is that the player began her run from an onside position. This simplifies the thinking process when a rapid decision is required, based on missing information. In this case, experience at a particular level of play is influential for assessing plausibility."

"In support of the position that availability heuristics are employed, a frequent error cited for new Canadian Football League officials making the transition from Canadian University level officiating is underestimating the abilities of the players, given the large jump in the skill level of the athletes. Offside is a particular judgment in which the newly transitioned official may reason that the player 'could not have been that fast.' In fact, at this new level, the player's speed is a plausible attribution for their positioning. The lack of sampling of these skills, however, makes the new official vulnerable to this judgment error. In this case, experience will eventually contribute to the availability heuristic that is used to fill the information gap."[22]

Context Matters

Any game in any sport at any level is a dynamic, roller-coaster of momentum, emotions and skill. While playmakers can manage this pendulum swing better than others, their efforts rise to the occasion to win the game. An official's focus on keeping the game fair and safe must match the intensity of every player's action. While studies of past game data show a referee's history of calls during these times, we need a framework to understand them.

Years after her article with Bill Mildenhall, Dr. MacMahon has continued to study the decision-making behavior of officials. In a 2020 paper[23] with renowned sport science researchers Dr. Markus Raab, Dr. Simcha Avugos, and Dr. Michael Bar-Eli, they presented a decision-making model to explain when officials recognize that a game has crossed an intensity threshold and they must switch to a stricter style of officiating.

First, officials in different sports have varied roles. To

start their analysis, the researchers sorted referees, linesmen, umpires and judges into three categories, interactors, monitors and reactors. Interactors, such as basketball, hockey or soccer referees have, obviously, a higher rate of interaction with players making direct decisions about their behaviors. Monitors, such as gymnastics or diving judges, assign a score to an athletic feat but rarely converse with the athlete. And reactors make a difficult but often black or white call, like judging a ball as in or out. In team sports, our focus here, the interactor referee is our focus.

To understand the burden put on these referees, a study[24] of the 2000 European Championships in soccer showed that they make an average of 44 observable calls (whistle blown for an offense) and another 60 decisions where they decided not to make a call and allow play to continue. Given the actual game time duration, that is about 3 to 4 decisions per minute, a demanding perceptual-cognitive load.

As with playmakers, officials face situations that require instant reaction (foul or no foul) based on the visual information they processed and their knowledge of the rules. Judging a foul is often a subjective decision based on severity of the contact and how it affected play.

One theoretical framework that has a long history of usefulness in these scenarios is Decision Field Theory (DFT). As time passes, the attractiveness of different options change based on extra information and confidence towards each choice. The first option that crosses a pre-determined threshold is the chosen one.

Think of a quarterback surveying his receivers after the snap of the ball. As they move away from the line of scrimmage, each one will have varying levels of probability of catching a pass thrown to them. Some are covered tightly at the line but then break free after five yards. Others may be open immediately, but then the window closes as the defender closes in. For the quarterback to pull the trigger, one receiver has to cross a threshold of probability that satisfies the quarterbacks' risk/reward determination. If none reach that point, the QB will decide to not throw and scramble downfield instead. At the time of the snap, the options were roughly equal but with each passing half second, the payoffs of each receiver change producing an "affective reaction" or valence to each choice. If the valence for one passes the QB's confidence threshold, his arm will fire the ball in that direction.

"The model describes how a person's preferences evolve across time until a decision is reached," wrote the researchers. "The model is used to predict how humans make decisions under uncertainty, how decisions change under time pressure, and how choice context changes preferences."[25]

Just as DFT works to explain a playmaker's decisions in a single play, Raab, Avugos, Bar-Eli and MacMahon contend that the same timeline-based model can apply across an entire game for officials. Each referee has their own threshold to trigger a whistle. Some may be more strict interpreters of the rules, less inclined to game management. They will have a lower threshold for a foul and call a tighter game.

The distinction is between adequate and accurate decision-making. Games that are getting out of control or balance may need to step back to adequate officiating with an emphasis on game management. Less emotional games can stick closer to the letter of the law with calls that reflect more black and white decisions. But "adequate" officiating can be a slipper slope. With high emotions come more agressive fouls and heated exchanges. And if the two teams have a best of seven playoff series in front of them, things may escalate into a flurry of technical fouls. How do players react in that environment? Let's take a look.

Strategic Fouls

Even for NBA playoff basketball, the 2020 opening series between the Dallas Mavericks and the Los Angeles Clippers was ill-tempered and physical. While the favored Clippers featured two-time NBA Finals MVP Kawhi Leonard and five-time All-NBA teammate Paul George, the Mavericks showcased their future in Kristaps Porzingis, a 25-year-old, 7'3" Latvian center who was the fourth overall draft pick in 2015, and Luka Doncic, the 21-year-old point guard from

Slovenia who was the Mavericks first-round pick and third overall in the 2018 draft.

A superstar pairing versus a next generation duo. After spending weeks in the pandemic-induced quarantine bubble in Orlando, the tension of the playoffs combined with the stress of isolation, confinement and fatigue to create an atmosphere ready for fireworks. The pundits expected a quick series win for the second-seeded Clippers over the seventh-seeded Mavericks. But the Mavs' young point guard had other plans.

Among the established and rising All-Stars on the floor, Marcus Morris Sr knew his role on the Clippers. An NBA veteran of eleven seasons, he provided the muscle inside, set screens, grabbed rebounds and shot the occasional three-pointer, all with a street fighter's intensity. Tied for the 2020 season league lead with 16 technical fouls, Morris was never shy to express his opinions to opponents or officials.

Doncic, who collected his own impressive total of 13 technicals in the same season, provided the brash but brilliant fuel to stoke Morris' temper, starting with game 1. On his way to scoring 42 points in his first NBA playoff game, Doncic was called for traveling in the second half. Morris tried to grab the ball out of Doncic's hands to inbound quickly but the Mavericks point guard resisted. A scuffle ensued with Porzingis stepping into the fray to protect his teammate, giving Morris a shove and receiving his second technical of the game, sending him to the bench. Despite Doncic's heorics, the Mavericks lost the game.

Even more intense in game 2, Doncic quickly scored 28 points but also committed his fourth foul early in the third quarter then his fifth early in the final quarter, allowing him only nine total minutes in the second half. With Porzingis' strong play, the Maverick evened the series with a win. Despite becoming the third youngest player in NBA playoff history to score a triple-double (double digits in points, rebounds and assists), Doncic twisted his ankle in the third quarter limiting him to only 13 points, resulting in another Mavericks loss. Along the way, he and Montrezl Harrell, a Morris-sized power forward, exchanged angry words giving them both a technical foul.

Coming back on a gimpy ankle in game 4, Doncic quickly picked up another technical foul in the first quarter for complaining to the officials about the rough treatment he was enduring from the Clippers. The game went into overtime where Morris landed a 3-point shot with only nine seconds to take the lead with a potential game winner.

But Doncic, who already completed his second consecutive triple-double, launched a shot with time expiring from well beyond the three-point arc. As the buzzer sounded, the ball swished for Doncic's 43rd point and the victory.

"I was just trying to make it," said Doncic after the game. "I can't explain the emotions I had, not only when the ball goes in but when I see the whole team running toward me. That was something special, one of the best feelings I've ever had as a player. Just something special."[26]

"He's a guy that lives for these moments and is completely fearless," said his coach, Rick Carlile. "At the end, it was all about finding a way to get the ball in his hands."

With the series tied, the heat was on for game 5. Again, Doncic was being roughhoused by the Clippers and again he received an early technical call for protesting his treatment. The Mavericks' Tim Hardaway Jr scuffled with Morris, resulting in technical fouls for each. Then Hardaway swiped at Paul George's face to get his second technical and an ejection. Carlile later objected to another call and also received a technical.

Then, early in the third quarter with emotions high, Doncic was under the basket waiting for an inbound pass. Morris came up behind Doncic and stepped directly on the back of his left foot and ankle, the same one that had been bothering him throughout the series. Doncic's shoe came off and he winced in pain but no foul was called. Both sides accused each other, the Mavericks saying it was a deliberate, dirty act while Morris and the Clippers claiming it was an accident. With Porzingis missing his second game with a sore knee, the Clippers took advantage with a punishing 44-point victory to take the series lead.

Game 6 started with a bang. With a minute left in the first quarter, Doncic drove to the basket guarded by Morris. Their arms tangled up as Doncic tried to shoot but then Morris swiped his right arm down from behind Doncic, striking the point guard on the back of the head and sending him to the floor. He popped back up and had to be separated by his teammates and coaches from going back at Morris.

The Clippers forward was charged with a flagrant foul two, defined as "unnecessary and excessive contact by a player against an opponent," resulting in his ejection from the game. Later in the game, Doncic received his fourth technical of the series, tossing the ball a bit too hard back to the ref after being called for a foul. Despite Doncic's 38 points, the Mavericks played a third game without their star center, Porzingis, and succumbed to the Clippers in the game and the series.

After the game, each side had their opinions on the Morris ejection and the rough play during the series. "It was a terrible play," said a dejected Doncic. "What can I say? It's two games in a row he did something like that. I really hoped the first game it wasn't on purpose, but looking back on the foul this game, you know what I think."[27]

"They had to make that call," said Morris about his flagrant foul. "I think, honestly, we had a lot of back-and-forth this series. It was a hard-fought series. I just don't want people to mistake playing basketball, playing hard with trying to hurt somebody. He's a young player. He's going to be the face of the league. I've taken into account all of that. I have been around for a while. I know how this thing works. ... I am a grown man. I stand on my own. Like I said, I didn't mean to step on his ankle. They can say the stuff that they want to say, this and that, on Twitter. ...

Whatever they want to say, they can say it. I am going to continue to play, happy that my team is in the second round."[28]

"I don't think he should have been thrown out, but listen, I'm biased," Rivers said. "I thought he made a play on a ball, and he hit him on the head. It happens all game. I think it was a reputation throw out, but you've just got to live with it. I love Marcus's intensity. Yeah, he's a tough guy. He's not backing down, and I love that."[29]

With Doncic as a playmaker, this series seems to support the idea that intense players play better. While coaches should not condone physical play that is outside the rules, they can point to the passion and competitiveness as a key component to success. In just two seasons, the accolades for Doncic are from an impressive list of players and coaches, with a common thread to their compliments - vision.

Gregg Popovich, 5-time NBA champion head coach of the San Antonio Spurs: "I think [it is] his demeanor. He has a pace about him that is never frantic. He's calm in everything that he does. He understands spatial relationships and understands where everybody is on the court, what's needed at the time and he's got courage. He'll take big shots and do what needs to be done to try to win a basketball game.[30]"

LeBron James, 4-time NBA MVP: "I don't think [the NBA game] is intimidating to him. I don't think this game is something he hasn't seen before."[31]

Giannis Antetokounmpo, 2-time NBA MVP: "He's an

amazing player - he can find his teammates, he can create his own shot - high IQ player."[32]

Dirk Nowitzki, Dallas Mavericks center, NBA MVP and 12-time All-NBA: 'He plays with a savviness that I never had - I might still not have it. Honestly, the way he carries himself in scrimmages... the way he reads the situations in pick-and-rolls, passes, he's fantastic. His court vision is something that I haven't seen in a young player like that in probably forever."[33]

Different Types of Aggression

But beyond raw talent, let's look at the link between aggression and performance. Does a playmaker's intensity, as measured by rules and fouls, translate to improved statitical contributions to the team? Three recent studies approached the question differently but all through the game of basketball.

Back in 2011, Emily Zitek, assistant professor of psychology at Cornell University, and Alex Jordan, psychologist and adjunct professor at Dartmouth College, noted that aggressive behavior by athletes is associated with better game outcomes across several sports, according to research.

Specifically, in college hockey, McCarthy and Kelly[34] linked penalties for more violent actions (roughing, boarding, fighting, etc.) with higher numbers of goals and assistsm, while another study showed a correlation between number of penalties and wins.[35] But in reviewing these studies, they point out that there are two types of aggression for athletes, and the existing research did not set them apart.

"When an athlete intentionally harms another athlete but the ultimate *goal* of the action is not the harm itself, but rather the achievement of some other end such as victory in the competition, it is called instrumental aggression," write Zitek and Jordan. "A more substantively interesting question is whether aggressive behavior that is not aimed at any further goal—aggression that serves only the goal of psychologically or physically harming a target person—is associated with positive or negative performance outcomes in sports. Such behavior has been called hostile aggression."[36]

Using five seasons of NBA game data, the researchers drew a distinction between instrumental and hostile aggression by the type of fouls they chose to include, "We conceived the present study with the goal of utilizing a purer operationalization of hostile aggression than has been used in prior studies. For this purpose, we selected technical fouls in the context of professional basketball. Technical fouls are an especially strong indicator of hostile aggression because they are given out only for behaviors that do not directly contribute to the goal of the athlete."[37]

As hypothesized, there was a significant relationship between hostile aggression and performance. "Controlling for the season year, the number of minutes they played, and their position, NBA players who received more technical fouls scored more points and had a greater number of rebounds and blocks than did players with fewer technical fouls. Players with more technical fouls also had marginally more assists per season than did players with fewer technical fouls. A greater number of technical fouls was also associated with a greater number of field goals attempted and made and a (marginally) higher field goal shooting percentage. Furthermore, players with more technical fouls were better at getting to the free throw line, and therefore made more free throws, than did players with fewer NBA technical fouls (even though there was no relationship between technical fouls and free throw shooting percentage)."

It was not all positive news, as those with more technical fouls committed more turnovers and were less accurate from three point range. This suggests that a more aggressive player succeeds at basketball skills requiring power and high energy while hurting their finesse and control moves. And by looking at only technical fouls, which do not include physical contact during play (that's covered by flagrant foul rules), Zitek and Jordan isolated belligerent behavior, outside of instrumental or goal-oriented aggression.

But does this increased performance help win games? There is a definite energy shift after a technical foul is called and the opposing team gets a free throw and possession of the ball. Zitek and Jordan noted this need for follow-up to their study, "One major question for future research is whether aggression by individual basketball players helps or hinders the performance of the whole team. Aggressive players may score more points and do better overall than less aggressive players, but it is possible that their aggression harms their teams."[38]

We had to wait nine years to answer that question, but in 2019, researchers from Israel and Spain gathered data on 80 technical fouls from 65 international basketball games to find out more. But their study focused more on the idea that a technical foul could be strategic in trying to win the game, an example of instrumental aggression, rather than a purely emotional outburst, a hostile aggression.

They also differentiated between technical fouls given to players versus those given to coaches or personnel on the bench. Plenty of technicals are given to argumentative coaches complaining about a call, as we saw with Mavericks coach Rick Carlisle. But there are also technicals given for events like delay of game, calling too many time-outs, illegal defenses, etc that are not hostile acts but either tactical ploys or simple mistakes.

By examining the changes to the game, in scoring, turnovers, fouls and violations, for 1, 3 and 5 posessions before and after a technical fould is called, the researchers could conclude the true effects in team momentum and performance. Results showed the opposing team (not the fouling team) scored slightly more points during the first five possession after a technical but also received more fouls called against them.

The additional fouls may be due to the official's subconsciously balancing their technical foul call but the scoring deficit of the fouling team suggests that the individual advantage to aggressive behavior that Zitek and Jordan found may not help the entire team, as summarized in the second study:

"The results of the current investigation should be of substantial interest to coaches and players. While the previously reported findings by Zitek and Jordan showed that being overly aggressive to the point of receiving a technical foul could have positive results (e.g., earning points), our data suggest that being overly aggressive generally is disadvantageous for the fouling team from a mid-term performance (5 ball possessions) point of view."[39]

So, while committing an act of aggression on the basketball court my temporarily pump a player's adrenaline, as we saw throughout the Mavericks-Clippers series, the team may ultimately suffer. Interestingly, in a 2020 study,[40] German researchers wondered if personality type was tied to a tendency to foul.

Across 242 top, under-19 German basketball players, they tracked a season of fouls with the individual results from the HEXACO personality questionnaire given during pre-season. HEXACO is an acronym for the six type classifications identified by the assessment; Honesty-

Humility, Emotionality, Extraversion, Agreeableness, Conscientiousness, and Openness to Experience.

The only trait that had a statistically significant correlation with fouls was Conscientiousness. Described by the contrast between the adjectives "organized, careful, precise" versus "sloppy, reckless, irresponsible", those high in Conscientiousness committed fewer fouls, of all types, than those low in this trait. Not even Honesty-Humility, a rather obvious trait for playing by the rules, was not linked to the quantity of fouls committed.

Without rules, there is no sport, just mayhem. Even with rules, sports can get emotional and complex. While the rulebook may seem like a constraint, the playmaker, along with a clever coach, not only understands the rules but may use them along with time to create tactics that provide a competitive advantage. That strategic plan of attack needs to be balanced with the playmaker's creativity, which we will learn next.

6

TACTICS

"Tactics are so important because everybody has to know what they have to do on the pitch. Our job is to convince guys that our way is the best way to cross the road."

— PEP GUARDIOLA

In any sport, winning tactics are rare and master tacticians are even more sparse. It is the coach's role to organize the players into a single, cohesive unit to "cross the road" together, as suggested by Pep Guardiola, manager of Manchester City FC of the English Premier League and one of those tactical masters of the last decade.

Coaches must coordinate formations, movement,

responsibilities and even creativity or a team will disperse in as many different directions as there are players. In continuous motion sports, like soccer, the chessboard is dynamic with all players in constant motion. As soon as the whistle blows, a team notices the subtle differences in their opponent compared to how they looked on the game film they had studied. Static X's and O's on a whiteboard are now shifting and changing their positions, not nearly as predictably as once thought. No longer in a pre-planned, controlled environment, players now must react to what their senses are perceiving.

When this happens, do tactics get lost in the player's memory? How do players correlate the logical plan they heard from their coaches in training to what is happening in front of them? How does their brain overlay the tactics template on top of reality? In this chapter, we will look at these questions and how they relate to a playmaker's decision-making.

Everyone Has a Plan Until...

One of René Marić's favorite quotes is from Mike Tyson - "Everybody has plans until they get hit for the first time."[1] The often misquoted quip, one of the former heavyweight boxing champion's most famous, is regularly repeated in locker rooms during fiery halftime speeches. In response to reporters who told him that Tyrell Biggs had a plan to beat him in the 1987 bout for the undisputed heavyweight title, Tyson uttered his famous line, not to discount planning but to know that plans need to be flexible.

"That's football, too. You can go out with certain ideas of how you'll play," said Marić, the 27-year-old assistant coach of Borussia Monchengladbach football club in Germany's Bundesliga. "Then the opposition react, change the way they attack the ball or position themselves, and you have to change in response. It doesn't always happen because of the manager, either. Sometimes, a player realizes he needs to be four meters to the left to close a gap and by that simple act, he solves a problem for his team and creates a new one for the opposition. There are infinite decisions made in a game of football. It's impossible for the coach to make this decision for the players. We can give them a guideline or a 'solution space' through principles, they have to perceive, decide and execute on the pitch."[2]

Marić's meteoric rise in the coaching world comes from his fundamental understanding of tactical methods and the advanced analytics used to measure them. Four years ago, he was coaching youth soccer in his tiny hometown of Handenberg, Austria. While in-depth, detailed discussions of soccer tactics might be possible at the local tavern, they most likely would stay there among the monogrammed beer steins.

But on the Internet, Marić's opinions, written in 5,000 word essays on spielverlagerung.de, the website he created with a few like-minded fanatics, reached a wider audience including professional coaches surprised by his uncanny insight into their own team.

Thomas Tuchel, who at the time was coaching FSV Mainz in the Bundesliga and is now the manager of superpower Paris Saint-Germain, was one of the first to inquire why a twenty-something fan, who only had access to game video and a few stats, could decipher his team's strengths and weaknesses with such clarity.

"Tuchel had seen one of our reports about his team and thought: 'That's pretty accurate, how did they know?' He invited us to Mainz and wanted to know our opinions: our views on the game, what we thought of their opponents, football things in general. We spoke for two hours and he gave us some small projects to see how we work and think. We did it for a season."[3]

Another fan of Marić's work was Marco Rose, who contacted the young Austrian when he was managing the under-18 team at nearby Red Bull Salzburg. Trading ideas for hours, Marić worked up the nerve to just blurt out his wish. "I thought: 'Hey, why don't I just ask?' We'd been talking about all sorts of things and then I asked: 'Next season do you need an assistant coach?' He [Rose] said: 'Yeah, let's try.' In the end, it worked out pretty well."[4] To date, that may be an understatement.

After winning the UEFA Youth League in 2016-17, the pair ignited their coaching rocket. The next season, Rose was promoted to senior team manager at Salzburg with

Marić by his side, winning the Austrian Bundesliga and appearing in the semi-finals of the continental Europa League tournament.

Next, it was another step up to Borussia Monchengladbach of the German Bundesliga, one of the top four leagues in the world, making Marić the youngest assistant coach among the 18 teams. During their first season in the global spotlight, The Foals, as the 120-year-old club is known to their fans, finished in fourth place, securing a place in next season's lucrative UEFA Champions League tournament.

While Rose has other, more senior assistant coaches and video analysts on his staff, he turns to Marić for tactical solutions and communication methods to his players. With a graduate degree in psychology, Marić understands that the players are the ones who execute the game plan and supplying them with ideas is the aim of coaching.

"For me, it's definitely not a specific match plan with pre-determined sequences, situations, or moves. In my mind, tactics describe the sum of a team's decisions about how they're going to solve a particular situation. Tactics is, for instance, a player recognizing where and how he is being closed down but still managing to still see an available teammate.

And also how that teammate has positioned himself in such a way to remain available, and then to receive a pass in the right place at the right moment. Ultimately, it's a very simple process: on the pitch, you're either protecting the ball, demanding the ball, or creating space. There is nothing else. Tactics is the mutual resolving of a situation through these actions by means of pre-defined playing philosophies, which correspond with the players' abilities and their understanding of the game."[5]

As coaches and even fans can see what seems to be obvious opportunities during a game, the view is much different for the players and, as we have been detailing in these chapters, more difficult.

"From the touchline, you're only virtually viewing the solution, which appears to be relatively clear," said Marić. "On the pitch, however, the player has to internalize all aspects of the problem and ask himself, 'Where can I play to? Can I play deep, diagonal, or across? Do I need to lay the ball off or is a quick switch available?' He has to review six, seven, eight solutions within seconds. The fundamental principles in football based on the initially mentioned actions are always the same, but you can derive patterns specifically for a position or the opposition."[6]

Unlike American football's designed and choreographed plays, open games like soccer, hockey and basketball leaves the door open for creativity among the framework of tactics, according to Marić:

"You can show them some concrete possibilities, dependent on the opposition doing certain things. It's an if/then decision process in some aspects. But no one says, 'OK, now it's play No 7.' It's more about saying that specific positional and numerical situations can lead to specific things. Every time players come up with solutions that we hadn't practiced, we're happier than they are.

It's great for a coach if the players get creative and come up with unforeseen answers within a framework. Then we can learn from them, which is cool. In some games, the opposition does exactly what we thought they might do and our ideas work out and in others, you need your players to make the right decisions."[7]

"It's about training them in such a way that will allow them to feel as little pressure as possible and to not lose the ball. That's because - on the field - it is the player who decides: if he feels that by taking another touch he will lose the ball, then he'll pass - and, in itself, that wouldn't be the wrong decision. You should trust the players to find the right decision within the principles of play."[8]

Much like a teacher introducing a variation to solving a math problem or the slant of a different author in the milieu of American literature, a coach must link what the players already know with what tactics will work best against the next opponent. There is a balance between taking advantage of the team's collection of personalities and skills, their "style of play" and adaptations needed to win a game. Even two England legends, one a manager and the other a player, don't always see eye to eye.

Wayne Rooney, the all-time leading goalscorer for both Manchester United and the England national team, recalled his doubt of the tactics used by his longtime manager, Sir Alex Ferguson, who has won more trophies than any other manager in the history of soccer. Winners of the 2008 Champions League final, Manchester United reached the final again the following year against Pep Guardiola's Barcelona squad.

Against the possession game of the Barça trio of Messi, Xavi and Iniesta, Ferguson insisted on keeping their attacking style of play. But Rooney had his doubts, although voicing his opinion to their fiery coach was not acceptable.

"I remember Alex Ferguson saying, 'we're Man United and we're going to attack, it's in the culture of this football club' and thinking, 'I'm not too sure about this'. I think all the players knew, deep down, it was the wrong approach, that we were abandoning the way that had brought us success in that 2008 semi-final — and sure enough, both times we got outplayed."[9]

Again in 2011, the same two teams met in the Final with the Catalans lifting the trophy again. Rooney had hoped the tactics handed down would be different for that game.

"But we lost two Champions League finals going toe-to-toe with Guardiola's Barcelona, by trying to press high and get round them, which was suicidal," said Rooney, who now plays for his boyhood club Derby County. "There is being true to the club, but then there's sitting back afterwards and thinking, 'we lost.'"

At the elite level of the English Premier League and German Bundesliga, the players often match their manager's expertise regarding the best game plan, as they have mastered the subtleties of the game. In fact, it is that tactical mastery that intrigues coaches, parents and even young athletes who want to know the secret to obtaining it.

Specifically, is the playmaker's superiority from the cognitive representation of the coach's plan, (i.e. how they index and store that information in their long-term memory), or is it from the speed of processing that retrieves it from its storage vault? And how does visual perception trigger ideas within the constraint of what the coach said is acceptable?

In 2015, a team of German neuroscientists and computer scientists interested in these same questions designed an experiment to isolate this process off the field. They knew that implementing tactics on the field required information combined with real-time application, as they explained in the opening to their paper: "Tactical skills describe the ability of certain players to judge and decide for upcoming game situations appropriately. Tactical knowledge does not just facilitate information processing, but also permits a target-related and purposeful adaptation of behavioral potentials to conditions in the environment. It seems necessary to store and access all relevant information and outcomes of the learning processes in tactical team cooperation as information in long-term memory (LTM). Thus, an athlete's performance on the pitch not only involves knowledge about task-specific information but also a learning-dependent modification of information."[10]

So, they gathered 20 inexperienced (less than four seasons) soccer players and 18 experienced (over 17 seasons) to conduct two experiments. First, they showed each group a series of diagrams of soccer situations frozen in time, much like a coach's whiteboard with one team depicted by red triangles and the other team by blue triangles.

One of the triangle players had the ball, and a solid line showed who they intended to pass to. A dotted line showed a possible run by a player. There were 12 total game scenarios depicting four common team tactics (three scenarios for each tactic); pressing, counter-attack, switching the ball to the other side of the field, and getting back on defense. This provided two offensive tactics and two defensive tactics.

Projected on a screen for the player volunteers to view, the first experiment showed two such game situations side by side. The researchers asked the players to compare the situation on the left, the "anchoring" situation, with the one on the right and asked "Would your team (always the blue team heading up on the diagram) require the same team tactic in both situations?" They wrote their answer as the situation on the right side cycled through the remaining eleven scenarios. Then a different, randomly selected situation would anchor on the left and the process repeated.

This process tested the player's ability to compare quickly two similar but not identical game scenarios and apply their understanding of the four team tactics.

The results showed what might be obvious results, but in a unique way. The novice players could only correctly distinguish the offensive versus the defensive tactics, while the expert players could accurately sort each of the scenarios into the four specific team tactics. As predicted by the researchers, the expert playmakers compartmentalized or "chunked" a static image of player formations then generalized and classified the situation.

"Data supports the hypothesis that more experienced soccer players, as compared to less experienced soccer players, possess a hierarchically organized memory structure of team-specific tactics," wrote the researchers. "Less experienced soccer players' cognitive representation of team-specific tactics in soccer showed a clear separation of tactics related to the playing direction (i.e., offense or defense)."

"In contrast, the more experienced soccer players showed a functional organization of team-specific tactics in soccer that are aligned to the four soccer-specific tactical concepts (counter-attack, pressing, change sides, and back to defense) investigated in this study. These four tactical concepts form separate clusters in the long-term memory of more experienced soccer players. Independent units within the memory structure represent these team-specific tactics. In addition, more experienced soccer players connect the two defense and two offense tactics at a higher level. These findings suggest that this approach is able to indicate relevant cognitive representations of team-specific tactics in soccer."[11]

In the second experiment, they showed the same two groups of soccer players a single scenario diagram and asked them to select one of two team tactic options. So, with a diagram flashed on the screen, they might ask them to identify the scenario as a Pressing or a Counter Attack situation.

Not only were their accuracy and reaction time recorded, but an eye tracking system was used to focus on their gaze. The researchers predicted that the expert players would not only be quicker in choosing the right answer, but it would be because of a better visual process in surveying the scene, much like they do on the field.

As expected, the reaction time and score of the playmakers was better, but their gaze strategy differed from past studies. Other eye-tracking experiments showed that expert athletes used more fixations of shorter duration, in other words, their eyes focused on multiple points in the scene and moved around quickly.

However, in this experiment, they used fewer fixations of the same duration to beat the novice players in both reaction time and accuracy. By tracking the eye movements, they could generate heat maps of the examined areas down to how many pixels they viewed. Dr. Lex and his research partners explain:

"More experienced soccer players focused on selected spots within each match situation. Thus, the inspected areas are smaller as compared to less experienced soccer players. It seems that they know exactly where relevant cues for a proper decision-making are in the match situations. That enables more experienced soccer players to decide faster.

These findings add to the existing knowledge that experienced soccer players are better able to evaluate and prioritize a possible individual tactical behavior (e.g., passing options) than novices."

With eye-tracking technology slowly becoming more affordable, the researchers believe that more teams could use it to not only identify recruits with cognitive promise but also to develop underperforming players who excel in everything else.

One of those other areas that a young playmaker may show promise is creativity, which for some coaches is the opposite of following team tactics. But the dominant players over the years can see things differently and discover angles and patterns that others cannot. How creativity can mesh with tactics is what we will look at next.

"I Was Never, Ever Supposed To Be Here"

At the prime of his career, in the middle of his bookend NBA MVP seasons, Steve Nash became a playmaker under a microscope. In fact, Jack McCallum, the legendary Sports Illustrated basketball writer became an unofficial assistant coach for Nash's Phoenix Suns, given a place on the bench to observe and report on their 2005-06 season.

The result was several feature articles and a book, "Seven Seconds or Less—My Season on the Bench with the

Runnin' and Gunnin' Phoenix Suns."[12] The title phrase came from Head Coach Mike D'Antoni's innovative offense, emphasizing fast-paced ball movement led by a point guard who could shoot just as well as he could pass. It didn't work for D'Antoni in Denver, but when he became head coach of the Phoenix Suns in 2003, his priority was to acquire a rising Nash who was ready to return to the team that drafted him.

Embracing the three-point line or a pick and roll layup as a statistical preference over the mid-range shot, the Suns system of small ball took them to consecutive Western Conference Finals and three Pacific Division titles.

It was the dawn of a new era in basketball tactics, de-emphasizing the big man and showcasing fast, shoot-first offense that other teams slowly adopted (such as the Golden State Warriors who appeared in five straight NBA Finals, winning three of them). The D'Antoni-Nash connection was unique, pairing a creative system with one of the game's all-time creative playmakers.

And, almost twenty years later, they are partnered again as Nash, now the head coach of the Brooklyn Nets, hired his mentor D'Antoni as an assistant coach.

The numbers don't lie. Nash finished his career with the third most assists (behind John Stockton and Jason Kidd), leading the league five seasons in assists per game. And despite supplying 41% of all his teammates assisted scoring (fifth all-time), Nash was a deadly scorer when he did shoot. Only eight NBA players have ever achieved a 50-40-90 season (50% field goal percentage, 40% three-point percentage and 90% free throw percentage). Nash accomplished the feat four times in his career and missed a fifth time by a single free throw.

Over an entire career, Nash is the closest ever to a 50-40-90 average in either the regular season or the playoffs, with a lifetime 49%-43%-90% and 47%-40%-90%, respectively.[13]

As with most game-changers, Nash was a contradiction, as McCallum pointed out, "He is a small man in a big man's game, a white man in a black man's game, a Canadian man in an American man's game, a long-haired man in a short-haired man's game, a political man in an apolitical man's game. He licks his fingers and smooths back his brown locks--and that's just in mid-dribble--and in warmups the former youth soccer player is more likely to pick up a rolling ball with his foot than with his hands. Nash looks like the dead-end kid who never gets picked for the hoops game and ends up hustling bets at the corner pool hall."[14]

This string of dichotomies defined Nash's life growing up in Victoria, British Columbia, Canada. In 2016, two sport psychologists from Simon Fraser University, Jack Martin and David Cox applied a new social evaluation tool called the Life Positioning Analysis (LPA) to the upbringing of the NBA Hall of Famer, "for the purpose of identifying sources of his athletic creativity and work ethic."[15]

Through a series of interviews with Nash, his parents and others who played a role in his pre-NBA development,

Martin and Cox grouped, summarized and explained how the skinny, white Canadian became one of the greatest basketball playmakers in the world.

Canadian biographer Charles Foran compared Nash to the other sporting icon of Canada, ice hockey legend Wayne Gretzky. "The two share much in common. Both seem able to visualize what will occur several frames ahead of everyone else and flip through scenarios before finding the right one to apply. Both manage this at high speeds and under extreme pressure, displaying what commentator Jack Armstrong calls the 'inner calm' of great athletes. Armstrong also believes Nash has a 'huge basketball I.Q.,' a genius-claim often made of Gretzky."[16]

In an interview with Nash, Martin and Cox asked him about the source of this creativity combined with the physical skill to make one-handed, no-look passes at full speed. "I think it's just—I hope this doesn't come off the wrong way—sounding conceited or arrogant, but that's just my reality. That's the way I'm experiencing things.... I don't play the game thinking, 'I'm a few frames ahead of you, buddy.' I just—that's where I am, and sometimes you might have to coax your teammates to spots with your eyes. But I never feel like it's an entitlement—that's just—that's the way I think. I really enjoy passing and finding angles and seeing ahead and being creative, and that way was very fulfilling for me since I was a kid."[17]

As a kid, Nash received a gift from his dad, former semi-pro soccer player John Nash, who provided positive support to his son but with a very specific type of compliment.

"My Dad was a creative player. He saw the subtleties in the game, the creativity, wit of a player. So when I was in the backyard with my dad playing soccer, from the time I was—could walk, he always—first of all he could recognize wit or creativity or vision or seeing something before it happened, and always stopped and pointed it out, for lack of a better word. He—so there was a value system created for me for being creative, for seeing things before they happened—for tricking people, for being cheeky or witty with your game.

And I just can't imagine that many kids are afforded that. Sure, there's many out there and they probably get it from the streets. But I had this person that valued those things that a lot of other parents probably had no idea what they were. So that and the creative side of it I think was really impactful for me. Whereas a lot of kids might have had a dad that would say something like, 'Man, you are really fast.' Or, 'You kick that ball really hard. Or, 'Great goal.' My dad didn't really value those things as much as what you perceived or what you created or how you expressed yourself."

"If you made a great pass he'd be, like—he'd put his arm around you after the game and be, like, "That was really, really great the way you were unselfish there and passed to your teammate when you could have shot.' And so to have that kind of value system, that was the currency. As a kid, you want to obviously impress your parents or gain their approval. … I'm sure that's a huge part of why I've formed the way I did."[18]

Part of the LPA process is identifying what are called "position exchanges," roles that can be interchanged as a child moves through life. From being a student of the game to a teacher of the game, from being a passer of the ball to a shooter of the ball, from being a follower to a leader defines their growth within their chosen field and in the wider expanse of their life.

"They become capable of integrating and applying different instances of position exchange and coordination across an increasingly broad range of circumstances and situations," write Martin and Cox. "Material artifacts (e.g., basketballs and gymnasiums) typically are involved in such exchanges and interactions, but what transpires in these exchanges also involves the interactors' adherence to sociocultural roles, routines, rules, and conventions (e.g., the rules of basketball and game strategies)."[19]

In his grade school years, Nash played mostly soccer, not making the move to basketball until the seventh grade. Playing midfielder in soccer is like point guard in basketball, so this first positional exchange succeeded because of the same skills required of a playmaker. As Nash explained to the researchers:

"I think having to use your feet, first of all. So there's a parameter set on you that is more difficult than using your hands. In order to use your feet to get the ball places, you have to think ahead because you don't have as much time or that real accuracy that you can have with your hands. In soccer, I think you have to already be thinking what you're going to do with it before it comes to you.

And so these are things that I don't think basketball players that grow up playing just basketball get as much of that training, so to speak. So it almost felt like cheating to start playing basketball. I could use my hands. I had all the same angles and possibilities and then some with your hands, than you had with your feet. And you could do things much quicker with your hands, so to speak. And so I think playing soccer and seeing all those angles and those passing options and space and other—and opponents colliding and ebbing and flowing and having to think before you got the ball was a kind of a hyper sort of training environment for basketball, being a playmaker."[20]

Other position exchanges emerged from the Martin and Cox interviews; the dual roles of playmaker and the "go-to" guy, teacher and learner, and insider versus outsider. When Nash was the heir apparent to the point guard position in Dallas, head coach Don Nelson grew frustrated with the extreme generosity and unselfishness of Nash. Based on the praise that he grew up with for getting assists instead of points, Nash was the ultimate teammate passing up shots that his coach knew he could make.

"Don Nelson insisted that I score," Nash wrote in his farewell letter to the NBA. "I always wanted to pass, but he said, 'It's damn selfish when you don't shoot.' Or, 'If you're a dominant, f*ing player — dominate!' He insisted that I be aggressive. That growth was a turning point in my career."[21]

"Nellie was really hard on me, but he also really believed in me," said Nash in a pre-Hall of Fame interview. "He had more belief in me than I did. It was him imploring me to score. And that was a fundamental building block for me, because once I balanced the playmaking with the scoring, it opened up everything for me and my teammates. My nature is just to pass, pass, pass — to give. Nellie finally got it in my head that that was B.S. — that you're hurting us by doing that. He challenged me, without exactly saying it this way, to realize I was being selfish."[22]

The challenge worked, as Nash learned to balance being a playmaker with being the scorer. Nelson saw the difference immediately, "I didn't ask him. I told him he had to change or I was going to stop playing him. I told him, 'You're one of my best shooters and you won't shoot — I don't understand.' So I told him I was going to fine him every game he didn't take at least 10 shots. I definitely hurt his feelings, but he tried to change after that. He became an All-Star and didn't stop until he won two MVPs."[23]

Not seen in the development of playmakers is the endless hours of individual practice away from coaches and teammates. Grueling sessions of 500 jump shots and 500 free throws taught Nash the fine details of technique, which he could then bring with him to team practices and be an example for others. Martin and Cox conclude that this position exchange of individual learner to eventual teacher benefited not only his team but also his own creativity.

"By alternating between team play and individual practice, and working closely with coaches and teammates, Steve could internalize the positions of teacher and learner. This allowed him to analyze and determine his own strengths and weaknesses, and to work tirelessly to build on the former and improve the latter. This self-direction or self-determination became an important part of what motivated him to succeed and also offered a strategic approach to self-improvement."[24]

And as McCallum pointed out in his opening, Steve Nash was a study in the old Sesame Street game of "one of these things doesn't belong." But being an outsider fueled Nash to improve what he could, his cognitive game, his decision-making and the confidence to be the playmaker and the leading scorer.

As Kobe Bryant said about Nash, "Is he the fastest guy? No, but he's fast enough. Is he the quickest? No, but he's quick enough. Is he the tallest? No, but he's tall enough."[25]

And even without the physical gifts of NBA caliber, the mental preparation is ongoing throughout a career. "Certain players are predisposed to creativity and decision-making, and I guess I'm one of them," Nash says. "I do believe that, to an extent, point guards are born, not made. But you have to make yourself better. You have to take those natural gifts and expand them."[26]

Nash opened his Hall of Fame acceptance speech

claiming, "I was never, ever supposed to be here."[27] But as he told McCallum back in 2006, knowing that he was on the right road, "Most guys somewhere along the line will meet an obstacle they aren't willing to clear, whether it's shooting or dribbling or something off the court, like girls or partying. They will not keep on going. I kept on going. People have always told me that I'd fall on my face, that I wouldn't make it this far. But here I am."[28]

The Six D's

Besides the biographical analysis by Drs. Martin and Cox, the life of Steve Nash matches up well with another researcher's framework for developing tactical creativity. Dr. Daniel Memmert, Professor and Executive Head of the Institute of Exercise Training and Sport Informatics at the German Sport University in Cologne, Germany, believes that creativity is a trainable skill in young playmakers.

"You need the right methods and the right environment. Research over the last ten years gives us so many ideas how we can foster tactical creativity in the field. We have special time windows where it is easier and these time windows are early in life, for sure, especially until age 7 or 8. But, in addition, from our research, we know that later on when you are 16, 18, 20 or 24, you can still train tactical creativity. You can still enhance divergent decision-making and generate different kinds of solutions and creative answers during a match."[29]

The key phrase is "divergent decision-making", or the ubiquitous plea to "think outside the box", referring to the puzzle to connect nine dots, arranged in a box, with four straight lines that do not intersect. The only solution is to extend the lines beyond the assumed limitation of the box shape, hence the hint. Within the bounds of coach-inspired tactics, playmakers need to create ideas that "tend to be different" as the definition of divergent requires. Memmert explains that this is not only a cognitive feat but also a social experiment to see who has the confidence to try something new.

"At the moment, we are still concentrating on the person, to learn to generate a lot of solutions and then choose the kind of solution that is seldom and a little bit surprising for the opposite player. In the future, we can try to incorporate more variables, like society and other factors. We know that there are cognitive variables like working memory and attention. We know that when the player has a wider attention window, they will produce more creative solutions."

Memmert has developed six training principles specifically to encourage and build a junior player's creativity in a framework called the Tactical Creativity Approach, also known as "the six D's." The first four are especially useful for younger players in that 5 to 8-year-old age group while older players can also use all six.

Deliberate Play

Just as it sounds, games with no instructions and no structure reveal innate creativity as kids adapt to and manage the boundaries provided to them by their playmates. It is the backyard neighbors kicking the ball the around and inventing their own games with no adult interference (beyond basic safety supervision). It is in this stage that kids learn to love sports and discover their own skill set before the long years of being told what to do and how well they do it.

One Dimension Games

Also known as small-sided games, this is the next rung up the ladder in terms of structure. While instruction is still silent, the set-up of the game has some boundaries. Maybe it is a 3 versus 3 game with miniature goals or a ball juggling contest. As Memmert describes in an academic tone, "The main aim of one-dimension games is to have players learn divergent, tactical thinking in complex and dynamic situations, which means that they train single basic tactical components through a great amount of continuously repeating comparable tactical constellations."[30]

Diversification

One downside of early sport specialization is often burnout and overuse injuries, which are genuine problems with young athletes. But Memmert also argues that seeing similar situations through the lens of different but related sports will transfer across all of them. A young hockey defenseman will see scenarios that are both new and similar to what he has seen as a soccer defender, even though the object, a puck versus a ball, and the physical skills, skating versus running, are different.

As Memmert explains, "Therefore, for the generation of original ideas to sport problems, it is important that children and adolescents get into contact with different balls in their "ball game life" as early as possible, learn to control them with hand, foot, and tennis/hockey racket/stick, and think of situations in a different or new manner again. Thus, clubs and associations should encourage their coaches at an early stage, especially during the training of beginners and talent promotion, to train tactical creativity by using wide-ranging sport games that overlap regular training, letting the children learn to solve tasks with a variety of solutions."[31]

Deliberate coaching

We have seen them at many youth sporting events. The coach or parent who provides a step by step, pass by pass instruction set to their players during a game. Rather than allow them the chance to see opportunities, to create unique plays, they become like video game characters controlled by someone on the sidelines. Instead, Memmert suggests letting the player widen their field of view by not burdening them with a specific solution for every second.

"A wide focus of attention is necessary to perceive unexpected objects like unguarded teammates, which could be the starting point of original solution operations," writes Memmert. "Reduced instruction on the side of the coach leads to children and adolescents'—due to a wider focus of attention – more frequently being able to generate original solution possibilities with many variations than children and adolescents who were frequently confronted with attention-leading hints during practice. This suggests that the coach who continuously stops the training game and constantly gives tactical instructions to his youth players may not be designing their training for optimal creativity development."

"Generally, coaches have two possibilities to influence their players' scope of attention: directly through instructions, or indirectly by inventing forms of games or exercises that provoke a wider focus of attention for the players. Another training goal should be that the coach or teacher provides the children with the possibility to perceive and search for unexpected and (potentially) better solution variations through reduced instruction parallel to his own solution demands."[32]

Deliberate Motivation

When a coach inserts herself into training or a match, she can communicate in two ways, as Memmert describes, with a promotion focus or a prevention focus. Using a promotion focus, the coach can call on a player's hopes and dreams, creating a more positive and creative mindset. In a prevention focus, they almost give a player a guilt trip warning to not let the team down by making a mistake. Memmert writes that, "coaches and teachers should try to optimize the divergent thinking of the athletes with suitable promotion focus instructions ("my wish is that every third ball is kicked through gaps," not "I expect you to kick every third ball through gaps").[33]

Deliberate Practice

Finally, the last D is one that most coaches and players are familiar with, the need for a high quantity of quality practice. Whether or not the total practice time is 10,000 hours is less important, but a significant block of time in the first ten years of sport spent focused on both tactics and creativity is critical to a young playmaker.

"The quantity of hours of deliberate practice makes the difference between more and less creative team sport players, especially for top team players in the national teams. National league athletes began their specific sport later than players in the next highest level of competition. Therefore, deliberate practice seems to be an important characteristic for the support of tactical creativity, especially in later childhood and the beginning of adolescence."[34]

Revisiting the early years of Nash's sporting life, the six D's are apparent. Deliberate play and 1-dimension games were a daily part of his boyhood having fun with his brother and dad in informal kick-arounds in the backyard. By playing soccer, hockey and then basketball, Nash enjoyed a diversified "ball game" education, able to transfer skills between them. As Nash has described, the intelligent praise that his dad gave him about finding the open teammate and encouraging unselfish behavior was the deliberate coaching and motivation that instilled a lifetime of team-first attitude.

And the well-known stories of Nash's thousands of

hours of skill-specific training laid the foundation for tactical creativity, thanks to his working memory being freed up from monitoring his technical movement to full attention given to inventing one-of-a-kind flashes of brilliance on the court.

As Memmert concluded, "Recent empirical evidence based on the dual pathway to creativity model indicate that general working-memory capacity benefits general creativity because it allows people to maintain attention on the task itself and avoids unwanted mind processing."[35]

PART III

BETTER DECISIONS

7

MEASURING DECISIONS

"There are many things that you can't measure. But the great fun of what I do for a living is figuring out ways to measure things that people previously considered intangible."

— BILL JAMES

Daryl Morey wasn't quite sure how to describe the explosive growth of the event he was about to host.

"I always felt like we put a harness on a cheetah. I wish it was our brilliant sales technique, but honestly we caught a wave of people saying this could be really useful," said Morey, the longtime general manager of the Houston

Rockets and now the president of basketball operations for the Philadelphia 76ers. "I remember the early days, we were clearly topping ourselves in a big way every year, doubling. It reminded me of making a Pixar movie. Each one kept getting better, and we were like 'Holy cow!' And we've now gotten to where we're just happy to put out a solid 'Toy Story 4.'"[1]

Back in 2007, along with Jessica Gelman, CEO of Kraft Analytics Group, Morey turned a popular class they taught at MIT Sloan School of Management into a small gathering of 140 attendees. Moneyball, the book by Michael Lewis, had been published four years before while the movie version, starring Brad Pitt, was still four years in the future.

Bill James, the father of baseball's sabermetrics and, by extension, sports analytics, bridged that gap by being featured in the book, as a guest speaker at the very first Sloan Sports Analytics Conference (aka SSAC) and then mentioned prominently in the movie (Lewis is also a frequent luminary at the event).

Like the wild cheetah ride that Morey described, the SSAC has been on an upward trajectory for 14 years, squeezing in the 2020 edition just before the COVID-19 pandemic shutdown. Having outgrown the halls of MIT Sloan, the conference upgraded first to the Hynes Convention Center and then to the colossal Boston Convention and Exhibition Center.

Over 3500 attendees from 30 countries representing

over 130 professional teams and over 200 universities pack into ballrooms (including the Bill James room, named in his honor) to hear sports VIPs, including league commissioners, owners and athletes, converse about sports, the growth of sports, the business of sports and the future of sports. It's success has spawned several other likeminded conferences like the Sport Biometrics Conference[2] in San Francisco.

But the groundbreaking, data-infused insights which was the original intent of the conference happen in the side rooms with less than 50 chairs, all of them filled, as brilliant, somewhat shy, 20-something stats wizards explain their latest metric creation with alternating slides of mathematical formulas and data graphs followed by game video snippets of players proving the presenter's point.

In the annual competitive research paper category, the 2020 conference included study titles like "NBA Lineup Analysis on Clustered Player Tendencies," "Using Self-Propelled Particle Models to Aid Player Decision-Making in Soccer," and "PFF War: Modeling Player Value in American Football."[3] This year's conference theme of "Run the Numbers" seems to capture the essence of the intersection between sports and data analysis, according to Gelman, "Let's come here, learn how to run the numbers and also how to think more broadly about how you're going to apply it."[4]

For our purposes, we wondered if this explosion of sports analytics could help track the improvement of athlete decision-making. Surely, among the growing inventory of acronym adorned advanced stats, there would be a golden nugget of information that perfectly explained the playmaker's superiority.

As the management maxim goes, "what gets measured, gets managed" or its alternative "if you can't measure it, you can't manage it." But, unfortunately, Peter Drucker, the business management guru who has long been credited with that bit of wisdom, never actually said it.[5] Not that measurement of key indicators should be ignored, but sometimes they do not capture the essence of the issue.

So, in its place, Andy Grove, the pioneering CEO of Intel, built on top of Drucker's Management by Objectives philosophy with his own mantra, Objectives and Key Results (OKR). In his world, each employee has to understand the overall objective, the goal of the company, and then how their individual activities, the key results, supported the objective.

John Doerr, the famous venture capitalist and student of Grove's advice, summarized OKR in the title of his 2018 book, *Measure What Matters*. "The key result has to be measurable," said Grove in a 1975 OKR training video cited by Doerr. "But at the end you can look, and without any arguments: Did I do that or did I not do it? Yes? No? Simple. No judgments in it."[6]

So, just as athletes and coaches measure gains in speed, strength, endurance and other physiological markers, decision-making also needs a baseline comparative measure to gauge any improvement effort. Before coaches will try any new technology or training technique, they need to have a framework for judging its success.

Billy Beane, the Oakland A's general manager and protagonist in Moneyball, stressed to his veteran scouts that they were not measuring what matters. In fact, there was no measurement at all. It was all based on how a player looked, along with a few nominal numbers attached to his name. Beane agreed with the Bill James philosophy that creating runs mattered in baseball, and the only way to do that was to get on base. One of the well-known and most revered baseball statistics, the batting average, ignores walks, errors and being hit by a pitch.

As Michael Lewis quoted James in Moneyball, "Think about it. One absolutely cannot tell, by watching, the difference between a .300 hitter and a .275 hitter. The difference is one hit every two weeks. It might be that a reporter, seeing every game that the team plays, could sense that difference over the course of the year if no records were kept, but I doubt it. Certainly the average fan, seeing perhaps a tenth of the team's games, could never gauge two performances that accurately—in fact if you see both 15 games a year, there is a 40% chance that the .275 hitter will have more hits than the .300 hitter in the games that you see. The difference between a good hitter and an average hitter is simply not visible—it is a matter of record."[7]

By concentrating on new metrics that valued the actual objectives by recording the relevant key results, James and his army of admiring apprentices brainstormed innovative ways to describe player performances.

Yet, with all of this insight now at the fingertips of coaches and general managers, the request that we still get from them is to unlock that black box of player decision-making so it can be identified, recruited, trained and improved. That is the goal of the final two chapters; first, to suggest measurement tools for in-game decision-making and second, to give examples of training methods to improve.

Our objective, as Andy Grove would insist, is to focus on decisions by the players as the key results. What is a good decision? Can we compare a player's decisions across different opponents, venues, game conditions, coaches, and time? Can we summarize a team's decision success rate? There may not be a single, glaring decision-making stat in every sport, but we can change how we think about measuring performance so that we can design practices and tactics that win more games.

As Peter Drucker told one of his business consulting clients in 1990, "Your first role... is the personal one. It is the relationship with people, the development of mutual confidence, the identification of people, the creation of a community. This is something only you can do."[8] That sounds relevant to coaches, too.

While Moneyball introduced sabermetrics to the masses in the last 15 years, Bill James and his peers have been publishing newsletters, articles and books going back to 1964, starting with Earnshaw Cook's "Percentage Baseball." But the discipline did not gain traction until James began his annual Baseball Abstracts digest in 1977, which explained and expanded on Cook's work.

In 1972, Bob Davids, who James hailed as "the man who has done more for baseball research than anyone else living,"[9] formed the Society for American Baseball Research (the SABR of sabermetrics). With their 50th anniversary in 2021, SABR membership has grown to over 6,000 with an annual convention that rivals SSAC as the preferred destination of analytics aficionados.

However, while baseball is ripe with numbers to pick from, the game comprises primarily one versus one matchups, particularly pitcher versus batter. Fielding and base-running have their own subset of stats, but the timeless battle at the plate is where James and his army have focused most of their attention.

As Warren Spahn, Hall of Fame pitcher for the Milwaukee Braves, cited, "Hitting is timing. Pitching is upsetting timing."[10] Up at bat, a hitter must anticipate a pitch, as the quarter second he has to observe it is far too little time to purely react. Predicting what the pitcher might throw given the specific game situation requires a decision that touches on several of the constraints (time and tactics) and traits (attention, cognition and emotions) of the Athlete Decision Model.

Like a football safety staring down the quarterback

before the snap, a batter has a sense of what might happen, prepares for that possibility but must remain flexible to surprises, like a deep pass when a short run was expected or a change-up when a 98 mph fastball would be the logical choice.

And while baseball is surely a team sport, its set-up is more aligned with single actions; a pitch being thrown, a batted ball being fielded, a baserunner deciding to advance. As a result, we can isolate these actions as discrete events, leading to them becoming well-defined metrics that describe past performances.

Still, our interest here is to study the actual decision made, judge its quality and then measure more of them over time as we make interventions to improve. While baseball does not have the continuous flow and team interactions like soccer, hockey or basketball, let's spend some time diving into a few stats to uncover the decision-making process of the hitter.

The Science of Plate Discipline

"The key to pitching is to have the ability to throw a strike when they're taking and throw a ball when the hitter is swinging."

— GREG MADDUX

The job of the hitter is the opposite of the pitcher's, as Hall of Fame pitcher Maddux expressed in the quote above; swing at strikes, not at balls. With everything else about the game situation neutralized, the imaginary strike zone is the rule constraint that hitters and pitchers play with.

If a pitch is inside the zone as it crosses home plate, the umpire should call it a strike, if not then it's a ball. If the hitter never takes the bat off of his shoulder, he can expect a walk to first base after four balls or the walk of shame back to the dugout after three strikes. If he decides to use his bat, he'll have much better luck swinging at a pitch in the strike-zone, although some hitters do well connecting with balls all over the plate.

Whether he gets on base with a walk or a hit made little difference to Billy Beane or Bill James because a player on base can score a run. A player trudging back to the bench after a strikeout or putout has zero chance of crossing home plate.

So, the sub-second decision of whether to swing the bat at a pitch is the spark plug to every other event in the baseball engine. Contacting the ball is critical, but it starts with making the choice, triggering the go sequence to the rest of the body.

Tracking a player's on-base percentage tells us more than looking at a player's batting average. But when the goal is improvement at the plate, we need to drill down even deeper into the decision matrix to discover what exactly is going well and what needs work. For a player who strikes out more than his teammates, is he swinging at strikes and not at balls? Or, more likely, is he trying to hit pitches well out of the zone or watching fat strikes go right by into the catcher's mitt?

This sub-science of hitting stats, known as "plate discipline", has opened up a new level of analysis. In Andy Grove's parallel sports universe, getting on base is the objective and plate discipline measures the key results.

First, let's talk about the data. Many of today's analytics tracking MLB players come from technology installed in the stadiums or worn by players that produce mountains of data points about the physics of the sport.

From 2006 to 2016, Major League Baseball used PITCHf/x from Sportvision in all of its stadiums. Using three high-speed cameras, the system provided data on the speed and movement of the pitch on its path to home plate. This data revolutionized both pitching and hitting analysis to within one mile per hour of speed and one inch of location.

Even so, in 2017 PITCHf/x was replaced by the TrackMan system that uses Doppler radar technology combined with OERT (Optically Enhanced Radar Tracking) as part of MLB's overall Statcast data system. This goldmine of data is available to the public for viewing and download on MLB's Savant website[11], creating an environment that allows sabermatricians to brainstorm thousands of combinations of pitch and contact events. Every MLB team now employs analysis staff to pick through this haystack of numbers looking for a needle that will stick.

For plate discipline purposes, there are three sets of binary events for each pitch; the ball was in the strike zone or out, the batter either swung at the pitch or did not, and, for a swing, he either made contact or whiffed. In the analytics acronym soup, these are O-Swing% (swung at a pitch outside the zone), Z-Swing% (swung at a pitch in the zone), O-Contact% (contacted a pitch outside the zone), Z-Contact% (contacted a pitch in the zone), Swing% (swings per total pitches), Contact% (contacts per total pitches) and other scenarios like first pitch strikes (F-Strike%) and swinging strikes (SwStr%).

They create these micro stats to tell a story about the hitter's decision-making success. But each story is specific to the player. Alex Bregman, All-Star third baseman for the Houston Astros and 2019 winner of the Silver Slugger award, led the league last year in O-Swing% by only swinging at 15.8% of pitches outside the strike-zone. On the rare occasion that he did, he contacted the ball an impressive 72% of the time, which was 13th in the league.

Of course, the quality of contact between ball and bat also makes a difference. By tracking the physics of the batted ball, using stats like launch angle (the angle at which the ball comes off the bat), exit velocity (how fast the ball leaves the bat at contact) and even the sprint speed of the hitter, Statcast can compute what-if scenarios that tell us the outcome likelihood of that specific contact, disregarding any amazing defensive play in the field.

Let's say Mike Trout rips a line drive with an exit velocity of 93 mph and a launch angle of 23%, both close to his season averages. Statcast compares that to every other batted ball with the same characteristics and assigns it the average expected outcome (single, double, triple, home run). So, even if a left fielder makes a diving catch to rob Trout of an extra base hit, we still measure the quality of his contact; he can't do anything about an amazing play in the field.

Given this additional information, we can add on to plate discipline with the expected batting average (xBA) and expected slugging percentage (xSLG). In 2019, Trout led MLB with a .678 xSLG and was sixth with a .310 xBA. So, even though Alex Bregman beat Trout in every plate discipline category except Z-Swing%, Bregman's .465 xSLG percentage was 46th in the league, mostly because of his 89.3 mph exit velocity and 19.6% launch angle.

In either case, Trout and Bregman are exceptional

hitters in a professional league filled with technology costing millions of dollars. How do these advanced stats relate to developing players in high school or college? While these amateur ball diamonds may not have Trackman radar systems installed, a keen eye in the dugout or grandstand can at least track pitches and at-bats from an eyeball perspective of being in or out of the strike zone and the hitter's decision in terms of swings and contacts. Or, even simpler, the ratio of walks to strikeouts, (BB/K), is readily available across most box scores.

What is important is that players and coaches pick one or two stats that are reliable game to game, season over season to isolate an objective, getting on base, with specific key results, walks or hits versus strikeouts or putouts.

There are many more decisions to analyze in baseball. We can match this quick discussion of hitting with analytics for pitching, fielding, base-running and even managerial decisions. But to get us back to sports that are based on more team-oriented attack strategies, let's detour into the world of artificial intelligence, specifically machine learning and neural networks, and how some clever programmers are revolutionizing how we measure decisions on the field.

Just Ask The Ghosts

It was an odd but effective analogy that the Manchester United players heard that day from their manager. "I remember going to see Andrea Bocelli, the opera singer. I had never been to a classical concert in my life. But I am watching this and thinking about the coordination and the teamwork, one starts and one stops, just fantastic. So I spoke to my players about the orchestra — how they are a perfect team."

Sir Alex Ferguson, who won 38 trophies during his 26 years in charge at Old Trafford, recalled that particular pre-game talk to Anita Elberse, a professor at Harvard Business School, as part of a case study she created about his demanding but successful management style, albeit of a sports team rather than a company.

The symphony metaphor is appropriate for most team-based, invasion-type sports as only the unified efforts of all players create the desired result, whether it be harmonious music or consistent victories. "To me, teamwork is the beauty of our sport, where you have five acting as one," said Mike Krzyzewski, all-time wins leader in college basketball, who sounds much like Phil Jackson, owner of 11 NBA Championship rings, "the strength of the team is each individual member. The strength of each member is the team."

During a game, one player's movement influences not only his teammates' proactive adjustments but also the reaction of his opponents. A ball carrier's cut to the left instead of the right changes the dynamics of both teams. At the end of the game, it's interesting to know each individual's analytics, like distance covered, passes completed and shooting percentage, but it is vital to visualize the coordinated movement of the team to truly understand how games are won and lost. The outside defender, small forward or right winger may have had a particularly good or bad day, but their net effect on the ensemble matters.

For decades, coaches have relied on game film to recall and explain what happened. Watching the action on video gives a richer, realistic recap of the motion that static statistics can't provide.

More recently, combining film with a numerical analysis offered two important but distinct assessments that still require coaches to integrate. Today's attempts to bring together the analog fidelity of film with the digital accuracy of analytics has stalled. Annotating video clips with play data, which allows for easier searches and context specific stats, helps but provides no way to apply advanced tools, like artificial intelligence (AI) and machine learning, to the thousands of micro-movements and positional changes of players throughout a game.

In 2010, when Peter Carr and Patrick Lucey arrived at Disney Research, armed with doctoral degrees in computer vision and speech recognition, respectively, they planned to contribute to the technical broadcast end of both Disney and its subsidiary, ESPN.

"Patrick and I were interested in understanding the sports broadcasting process, i.e. what do the camera operators choose to look at, and what storylines do the commentators discuss?" Carr recalled in an interview.[12] "We quickly realized that any insights into this process required a thorough understanding of what was going on in the current match, and that existing statistical methods seemed inadequate for this task."

That inadequacy ignited a seven-year research agenda to move the sports analytics world to its next logical progression, measuring and analyzing team movement. The emergence of player tracking systems, like SportVU from Stats Perform, provided the raw "GPS" data to digitize motion. Introduced in NBA arenas in 2010, the SportVU multi-camera system tracks and delivers real-time X, Y coordinates of each player and X, Y, Z coordinates of the ball at a rate of 25 times per second. Now available for multiple sports, this goldmine of movement data is the fuel that analysts and programmers needed to digitize player logistics.

"We like to think about sports data as a method of reconstructing the story of a match," said Lucey. "With tracking data we can reconstruct the story in finer detail, and allow us to answer specific questions."

Lucey, who transitioned from Disney to lead Stats Perform's data science team, relishes the opportunity to dive into the sheer volume of data available. "While I had five great years at Disney Research, I always wanted to be able to work with teams and work with data from the source," said Lucey. "At Stats Perform, we have been around for over 35 years and have amassed the world's largest treasure trove of data. People probably don't know it, but when you search for a score on the internet or social media — there is a good chance that information comes from us at Stats Perform. In terms of tracking data, we also have the most amount of tracking data in basketball (over 5,000 games) and soccer (over 12,000 games)."

In sports like basketball and soccer, coaches repeatedly emphasize the search for space and time. Pick and roll or swing offenses strive to open up space momentarily for a shot in basketball. Switching the field with long passes to the opposite side gives soccer players time to move forward before defenders close the space. So, using the spatiotemporal data provided by player tracking allows coaches to measure the success of their tactics.

"For me, the common thread has been developing machine learning algorithms to better understand spatiotemporal data about human behavior," said Carr when asked about the purpose of their research. "Team sports is a fascinating example because you have several teammates cooperating in an adversarial setting against another team. There are lots of tracking data at the professional level which makes it possible to use advanced techniques like 'deep imitation learning.'"

Deep imitation learning sounds like one of those murky, out-of-control AI nightmare scenarios that Elon Musk keeps warning us about. But in Lucey and Carr's world, it involves teaching a computer simulation how coordinated motion of the best teams achieve the best statistical efficiency, known in the analytics world as "expected wins," or "expected goals".

"In many complex situations, it can be very challenging for a human expert to describe and codify the policy or strategy due to the granularity or fidelity of the situation," wrote Lucey and Carr, along with fellow CalTech researchers Hoang Le and Yisong Yue, in a paper describing the project presented at the 2017 MIT Sloan Sports Analytics Conference (SSAC). "For such tasks, we can use machine learning to automatically learn a good policy from observed expert behavior, also known as imitation learning or learning from demonstrations, which has proven tremendously useful in control and robotics applications."

While these expected value measures compare a player's performance to a league average, (i.e. the expected point value for a certain player in a certain game scenario), coaches and athletes would often prefer to know how the movement of all the players created the time and space opportunity for that shot. Through brute force, using seasons worth of data, these algorithms learn the subtle positioning of players that produces the best result, not through real human intelligence of the game but an artificial yet effective intelligence.

"One crucial insight from our research is that a

computer must have a framework for anticipation," said Carr. "When machine learning algorithms only react to the current situation, without considering cascading effects, the results are clearly below what humans can do. However, we have been able to predict how specific teams will defend in different situations."

The Disney team took inspiration from the work of the Toronto Raptors analytics staff who spent five years painstakingly loading and programming SportVU data to not only show what Raptors' players did in a past game but also to predict what they should have done to more effectively counter an attack.

Imagine a coach's whiteboard with a diagram of the court. Now add different colored dots, one for each player on each team, red for the Raptors and blue for their opponents. Using just the historical SportVU positional X-Y data, they can put the dots into motion in a time lapse sequence showing a particular play. This would not differ from watching the actual game film, just substituting dots on a screen for the actual players.

But then the magic happens. From a defensive perspective, coaches know the actual result of the play from film, but they may ask "what should we have done?" And since excellence breeds imitation, they may also be curious what the best defensive team in the league would do in that situation.

What if we could add a third set of players or dots to the screen that simulate the best movement pattern to defend that play? Each actual player could compare their movement with the ideal movement as the play unfolds. These "ghost" players would represent an optimized defensive team that they players could mimic in practice drills.

And that's exactly what the Raptors staff did. As Zach Lowe described in a Grantland article,[13] "In simple terms: the Raptors' analytics team wrote insanely complex code that turned all those X-Y coordinates from every second of every recorded game into playable video files."

And that third set of dots shown on the sample video the Raptors provided?

"Those are ghost players, and they are doing what Toronto's coaching staff and analytics team believe the players should have done on this play — and on every other Toronto play the cameras have recorded. The system has factored in Toronto's actual scheme and the expected point value of every possession as play evolves. The team could use that expected value system to build an "ideal" NBA defense irrespective of the Toronto scheme."

Unfortunately, the tedious, manual data entry and annotation was very time consuming. So, the Disney team set out to help automate the process with a data-driven approach using a season's worth of tracking data. By feeding millions of data points into learning algorithms, they uncover the logic of the next movement, much like AI systems that have learned how to play a game of Go or chess.

Thanks to their access to 100 games of English Premier League player tracking data, they focused on "ghosting" an EPL team's defense, using about 17,400 sequences of attacking-defending game clips.

Just as the Raptors' staff had done manually, Lucey and Carr's team could model what a "league average" team of defenders would do as compared to the actual reactions of a single team. Better yet, they could also isolate and ghost how the best defensive team in the league would react to the same attacking play. For both the actual defenders in that game and the league average ghosts, their expected goal value (EGV), the probability that they would score a goal, was a disappointing 70%. But when using the ghosts of the league's best defenders in the same scenario, the EGV dropped to about 40% thanks to more proactive defending decisions.

As the volume of player tracking data grows, so does the what-if possibilities. Other recent insights from the Disney team have been that soccer teams position themselves higher up the field in more aggressive formations while away teams take a more conservative, defensive approach. Whether that bias is intentional is for the coaches to discuss, but Lucey and Carr have an idea.

"Utilizing an entire season's data from Prozone from a top-tier professional league, we used our automatic approach to see whether the formation they played had anything to do with explaining why teams are more successful at home rather than away," said Lucey and Carr. "Our analysis showed that nearly all teams tend to play the same formation at home as they do away, however, the way they executed the formation was significantly different. Specifically, we were able to show that at home, teams played significantly higher up the field compared to when they played away (or conversely, teams sat much deeper at away games). This conservative approach at away games suggests that coaches aim to win their home games and draw their away games."[14]

And while expected goal statistics tell us the probability of a scoring chance, coaches would still like to know the contributing factors leading to those opportunities. Again, the tracking data revealed the influences on a season's worth of shots taken in the EPL.

"From the data, we analyzed the spatiotemporal patterns of the ten-second window of play before a shot for nearly 10,000 shots," said Lucey and Carr. "From our analysis, we found that not only is the game phase important (i.e., corner, free-kick, open-play, counter attack etc.), the strategic features such as defender proximity, interaction of surrounding players, speed of play, coupled with the shot location play an impact on determining the likelihood of a team scoring a goal."[15]

And when they looked at over 20,000 three-point baskets from the 2012-13 NBA season, more clues emerged on how teams get their shooters open, which, unsurprisingly, raised their percentage. One interesting movement feature was the number of times a defensive team swapped their roles when switching who they guarded.

"We compared many different offensive and defensive team factors, such as team area, distance ran, velocity, acceleration, dribbles, possessions and passes — as well as our new role-swaps measure," said Lucey and Carr. "We showed that only the defensive team factors such as team distance, velocity, acceleration and role-swaps were predictive of the offensive team getting an open shot (in addition to dribbles and possessions), and showed that the type of role-swaps that occur are also informative of how a team gets an open shot (e.g. point-guard switching with the small-forward)."[16]

Explaining all of this wizardry to coaches may get plenty of blank stares, not because they don't understand the logic but that they're uncomfortable with a computer making decisions and instructing players on proper team movement. Lucey and Carr have seen those indifferent reactions before and have learned that they must sell their technology as a tool that coaches have available rather than compete with their years of "seeing it with their own eyes."

"We have to be careful of what tracking data can give us and more importantly what it can't," said Lucey. "There are limits of tracking data as it is just the center of mass (i.e., dots moving around). Instead of automating analysis, we think the sweet-spot is to build technology which helps a domain expert to their job better — create assistive tools for domain experts. Examples could be retrieving plays in video quickly, or highlighting key patterns of play of a team/player."

"The coaches/analysts have a great intuition on what is occurring. Technology should be able to help them quickly check these aspects. The important thing is not to tell people their jobs — they know it really well and is why they are in those positions. But we can help them do their job more efficiently. That is the big goal of my data-science group — creating technology to do this."

While SportVU cameras are still expensive enough to limit their use to top pro and college teams, wearable trackers might be a possibility for the mass market of teams at the high school and club level.

"Radio frequency identification trackers (RFID) generate similar, but also very different data," explained Carr. "Because they are on the body of athletes, there is the potential to measure other information like heart rate. But, unlike camera based systems, RFID only returns the location of the tracker (and any auxiliary data that can be sensed locally by the device). You don't get the same fidelity of information that is available in a video stream, like seeing the body pose of a player (or at least which direction they are facing)."[17]

Still, Lucey thinks the ubiquity of personal fitness trackers are here to stay.

"Non-pro athletes that have wearables on their body, like Fitbit, that capture the location and physiological data are becoming commonplace. Something that we are very excited about at Stats Perform is the ability to capture tracking data from any type of device and process it to do analysis."[18]

Even game video shot from a basic digital camera may soon extract data on movement and even body kinematics.

"Computer vision has improved so much, where this is actually a feasible thing now. We had a paper at a recent SSAC conference, from our very talented intern, Panna Felsen from UC Berkeley, that looked at how we can potentially use the body-pose estimated directly from a broadcast view, to conduct shot analysis. We did it on NBA players, but you can imagine that this could scale eventually to non-pro scenarios."[19]

One outcome from the Harvard case study on Manchester United's Ferguson was a list of his management methods, what Elberse dubbed, "Ferguson's Formula." In it, he recalled when he was a junior manager at one of his first clubs, Aberdeen in Scotland. His assistant manager asked for a larger role in the team's practice sessions, as Ferguson was running everything on the field. At first, Ferguson fought the loss of control but then realized that stepping back and observing the team from new angles opened up new insights into their play.

"As a coach on the field, you don't see everything," said Ferguson. "I don't think many people fully understand the value of observing. I came to see observation as a critical part of my management skills. The ability to see things is key—or, more specifically, the ability to see things you don't expect to see."

That's exactly what Lucey and Carr are trying to provide to teams, coaches and fans, an opportunity to see things you don't expect to see.[20] While Carr has moved on to Argo AI to work on self-driving car technology, Lucey now leads the AI team at Stats Perform which is creating the next generation of AI-assisted player analytics products.

But rather than creating new, mashed-up version of stats, Lucey is treating athletes like creative, moving human beings. "I don't actually think new metrics is the way to go," Lucey said. "I don't think that's the future. I think it's a symbiosis between a human and a computer. So can we develop new technology to help a domain expert do their job better? I think that's really the next step in sports analytics. Just enabling, creating this kind of technology just to help coaches or analysts or people at home to be able to ask these what-if questions. I don't think we're that far off."[21]

And that's what he and his group have done with introducing a service product they call AutoSTATS, which captures player movement data but does not require the pricy infrastructure of SportVU cameras. By taking advantage of years of computer vision machine learning research, the system can watch broadcast quality game video of different sports and track the x, y coordinates and a new feature that, according to Lucey, will change the game again.

"In basketball, in the player-tracking data, you only have two dimensions of the players," said Ben Alamar, a data scientist and former director of analytics at ESPN. "And so I don't know the direction those players are facing. I don't know if one of them is contesting a shot with his hands up. I don't know if they're jumping. Computer vision, if done in a complete way, gives me all of that."[22]

In today's tracking systems, the players are two-dimensional dots on a screen scurrying around the virtual court or field. As an information source, it's interesting because that directional information can convert to data. But what Lucey is developing is a way for the computer to also "see" details about the player's body positioning in sub-second detail. So, yes, he may have been "open" for a pass with no defenders around him, but he was facing away from the ball. Or, he may have stumbled and was trying to get back to his feet, something the x, y coordinates cannot communicate.

But now, OpenPose, a system developed with Carnegie Mellon University, can superimpose stick figure skeletons on top of the players in the game video and digitize their body pose, including the direction they're facing, positions of their arms and legs and vertical changes like jumps, falls or just a bend in the knees. While motion analysis has provided kinematic motion analysis for a while, being able to extract the skeletal details of each player from just a broadcast quality video feed is the big news.

"Once upon a time, we could capture body pose, but we

had to do that in a lab setting," Lucey said. "Now we can actually do it in the wild. The big thing — and this is what we can do really well — we can contextualize the data. You can ask us specific questions. You can say, 'Well, what's the likelihood of this player making that shot? Or, what happens if I switch that player with another player?'

"So, we can really do fine-grain simulations and ask those what-if questions.... We have the box score or we have these players' stats, but (I think the next stage in analytics) is to simulate these kinds of specific plays and see what a different player will do in these situations. In a given situation, we can model that context and we can give more precise answers because we understand the data in those situations."[23]

The biggest market for AutoStats, according to Lucey, is the digitization of hundreds of college games where there are no SportVU or similar player tracking cameras. With nothing but raw computing power, the AI can watch games, tag players, log their second by second movement, record body pose and then crunch and organize the data into usable reports. Each of these movements reveals clues about each player's decision-making, as well as their opponents. Recruiting players for the next level now goes well beyond simple stat searching. The system enhances opponent scouting to a deeper level of tendencies.

"Humans watch video, and then use their gut," said Lucey. "That doesn't really work. We want data-driven decisions.... Now we're doing it in a more effective way.

We're trying to emulate what a human does, but we're doing it to scale."[24]

Kirk Goldsberry, who earned a Ph.D. in cartography but now spends his time providing eye-popping analytics for ESPN, Team USA and his bestselling books, has been documenting the science of mapping out the basketball court to understand the movement of players between the lines.

"Space is such a key element of sports strategy and understanding," said Goldsberry. "In this decade, it's been the logical extension for sports analytics to start thinking and visualizing the spatial data." "Don't just tell me I'm a bad shooter, tell me *why* I'm a bad shooter," Goldsberry said. "Don't just tell me I'm an inefficient runner physically, tell me *why*."[25]

So, once again, to become a playmaker, a novice needs to make consistently good decisions. And to improve on both the consistency and the quality of those decisions, we need to present a before and after comparison.

Today's sports analytics continues to create novel combinations of numbers to describe what happened. Player tracking technology layers on the ability to not just report on actions taken but also understand the flow before and after an action. With the use of massive cloud computing power and search engines, available for a fraction of the cost of a decade ago, we can query databases for not just numbers, as Billy Beane and Paul DePodesta did for the Oakland A's, but also for video clip examples of similar plays.

After seeing a clip of an opponent's successful TD pass in their last game, a coach or player might want to query every play that team or any team has run similar in all aspects, including game situation, personnel attributes, defense called, and outcome. Instead of typing that in using text, the advanced analytics system will let you click on a button labeled "Similar Plays". Let the AI do the work of matching so that the coach or assistant avoids hours of research and the players get instant feedback to their questions.

But the challenge is for coaches and players to make that leap from data access to actionable knowledge. The data and media companies will happily offer a subscription plan to their vaults of organized data for us to search and sift to our heart's content. There will be no shortage of information available. Now, can we internalize all of this and call on it in a split second out on the field? Are budding playmakers merely exposed to this information, or are they truly absorbing it and learning from it? Will we see improvement over time, comparing the before and after metrics?

From Fighter Pilots to Quarterbacks

Brian Burke was asking the same questions, "The problem I was trying to solve was to find out how useful the player-tracking data could be. What kind of insight can we get from it beyond just the 'Tyreek Hill hit 22 mph on this play?'"[26]

After flying F18s for the United States Navy and solving strategy and tactics problems as a defense contractor, Burke (not to be confused with the hockey GM of the same name) turned his passion for football into a career. In 2007, he started the Advanced Football Analytics website where he created and explained concepts like in-game win probability graphics, a 4th-down go/no-go calculator, a win probability calculator, and an NFL Draft Prediction model.

"The Navy (unfortunately) taught me my statistics. They pulled me out of the cockpit, sent me to grad school, and for some reason thought it'd be a good idea for me to know a lot of multivariate regression. It was completely useless for me until I got out of the Navy and into football."[27]

After moving on to ESPN in 2015 to help build their football analytics insights, he embarked on a journey using AI, much like Lucey, to make this torrent of tracking data more relevant. At the 2019 SSAC conference, where he had become a popular speaker, he presented a research paper[28] about a tool he had developed, called DeepQB, that would try to answer the $40 million per year question, how do quarterbacks make passing decisions, or specifically, was their actual decision optimal?

"Optimal is the goal. I think we're close to optimal. I can't prove it. But it's doing several things. The first thing it does is it looks at the field of play. Where are the receivers? It looks at where the defenders are. It looks at what's going on with the quarterback. Where is he? Is he moving? Is he under pressure? It looks at not only the positions but the velocities, the orientations.

So, one of the great things about this data is there are two sensors on each player, one on each shoulder pad, and that gives us player orientation. And that is an important part of the equation. So, it looks at this field of play, it looks at the array of players, it looks at all the combinations of positions and velocities, and it can understand the play. It can act as the quarterback's decision-making function and say, who should I throw to, given this array of players. Who's open? Who's not? Who's further downfield? If I throw here, is it an interception risk?[29]"

By training a neural network with hundreds of NFL games and thousands of offensive plays, DeepQB can build an expected outcome for similar plays. Much like the xSLG or the expected goals in soccer, Burke's tool estimates the best outcome for a set of variables then compares a specific QB's decision and actual result to what we could expect.

Outperforming the expectation is the definition of an excellent decision. So, play after play, game after game, DeepQB can test performance by taking advantage of player tracking data at a computational level that no human ever could.

Despite the large number of variables on the field, Burke insists that the universe of options shrinks as the ball is snapped. When averaged over thousands of plays, (over 50,000 plays so far), the system simplifies the situation down to its core essentials.

"At the time he releases the ball, the time he throws the ball, there's a configuration of receivers and defenders. And the scheme of both his own team and the scheme of his opponent, as well as the skills, the speeds, the abilities of these opponents, are all captured within that configuration. So, we know the positions and the velocities, accelerations, orientations — everything these players are doing. And we can say, given that configuration, here's the expected outcome of this play. You know, you should make about a nine-yard gain, it should be completed, it should not be intercepted, and so on. Then we can look at what [he] actually did and make a comparison. So, if he is over performing what his team and what his opponents have presented him, then we can attribute that to [his] individual skill. So, in that way we're isolating quarterbacks' performance and quarterbacks' decision-making as much as we can."[30]

Burke admits that his system has miles to go before coaches will make it part of their training regimen, both because many coaches are slow adopters of new technology and because DeepQB does not yet truly "understand" the nuances of football. A neural network is a complex mathematical model, not a human brain.

There may be a reason that a receiver is open but Aaron Rodgers looks elsewhere, as Burke explains, "Was this a zone [defense] or was this man? That makes a huge difference in terms of separation. You could have a 3-yard buffer around you as a receiver, and in a zone you're covered. You could have a half-a-yard step on a quarterback as a wide receiver in man-to-man coverage and be wide open. So what I've learned is we have to take a couple steps back here and learn the context of these plays."[31]

These technologies are on a collision course. The enhanced player tracking extracted from HDTV video that Stat Perform's Lucey is developing combined with the decision-making optimization of tools like Burke's DeepQB will take us a step closer to measuring and comparing playmaker decisions.

Once we have this ability to show improvement over time, we can focus on the most effective training methodologies to speed up that growth. And that's what we will discuss next.

8

IMPROVING DECISIONS

"If you're a quarterback, you want everything on your shoulders. You want to be the one to make the decisions."

— TOM BRADY

F inally, we have arrived at the ultimate question, how can we train athletes to make better decisions during a game? So far, we have covered the components of our Athlete Decision Model, the traits and constraints that govern a player's decision-making ability. Athletes choose their next action based on what they pay attention to, their brain's unique capacity to process information and the ongoing battle with their emotional state. The game environment sets boundaries to their creativity by limiting the decision time available, enforcing the rules of the game and following the tactics set by their coach.

As with any improvement process, athletes need to measure progress starting before a training intervention until after a defined period to test what works. And that leads us to this last chapter on ideas for coaches and parents to use with their developing playmakers. Assuming you, the reader, did not just skip to this last chapter, tempting as it is, you now have an overview of these components of decision-making so that you can understand this generation of athletes better.

But first, let's talk about this generation. As with their parents and their grandparents, this cohort of kids is growing up in a different world with changing influences and expectations. Generation Z, (born from 1997 to 2010) is out there now on the fields and courts with a newly labeled generation right behind them.

What Comes After Z?

Mark McCrindle could see the dilemma coming from a decade away. As a demographer, social researcher and futurist, he studies generational changes and their socioeconomic impact. Having reported on the so-called

Generation X, Y, and Z, he pondered the nickname of the next batch of babies.

"The emerging generations these days sound a bit like alphabet soup," said McCrindle. "Just over a decade ago, it became apparent that a new generation was about to commence and there was no name for them. So I conducted a survey to find out what people think the generation after Z should be called."[1]

Back in 2005, when McCrindle put his survey online, there were so many Atlantic hurricanes that the usual practice of giving them Roman names from A to Z did not outlast the season. So, meteorologists used the Greek alphabet for the rest of the storms. That gave him inspiration to turn the page, even though "Generation A" was one of the popular responses to his survey. Moving forward into the 21st century was better than cycling back to the beginning, in his opinion.

"In keeping with this scientific nomenclature of using the Greek alphabet in lieu of the Latin, having got to Generation Z, I settled on the next cohort being Generation Alpha — not a return to the old, but the start of something new," said McCrindle.[2]

Just as members of Generation Y, (born between 1981 and 1996) are more popularly known as Millennials, this new Generation Alpha, (kids born after 2010), has also been nicknamed Screenagers or Generation Glass for their total immersion in screen-based technology.

"Generation Alpha is part of an unintentional global

experiment where screens are placed in front of them from the youngest age as pacifiers, entertainers and educational aids," said McCrindle. "They began being born in 2010, the year the iPad was introduced, Instagram was created and "app" was the word of the year, so they have been raised as "screenagers" to a greater extent than the fixed screens of the past could facilitate."[3]

As Millennials have more children, the boom of Generation Alpha will speed up. With over 140 million babies born worldwide each year, the Alpha group is expected to reach two billion by the artificial generational cut-off date of 2025. Along with the overlap of Generation Z, coaches will teach and train this contingent of kids for the next twenty years. But how different can they be? Despite the whims of marketing consultants to categorize and differentiate their tastes, habits and buying behaviors, are Generations Z and Alpha unique as young athletes?

Starting with Gen Z, now going through their teens and early twenties, the common misperception among their elders is that they have a shorter attention span. On the surface, this seems apparent. Rather than sit through a thirty-minute newscast, most in Gen Z prefer getting updates in headlines and quick summaries. Rather than watch a three-hour game on TV, they prefer to stream highlights of their favorite players. They multitask on their phone and tablets, jumping from one app to another to stay in touch with friends.

But this is less about lack of attention but more to do with quality of time spent. After all, this is the generation that binge watches entire seasons of their favorite show in one sitting. They are maximizers of their enjoyment per minute ratio. If something gets dull, they move on. Granted, the online environment that they live in encourages this in a self-fulfilling loop of content creation. Forward thinking sports leagues have embraced this reality in how they package their entertainment. While other sports have seen a decline in game ratings in the last decade, the NBA continues to grow its viewership, both in the arenas and through screens of all types, TV, laptops, tablets and, especially, phones.

"We promote the posting of our highlights," said Adam Silver, NBA Commissioner. "We analogize our strategy to snacks versus meals. If we provide those snacks to our fans on a free basis, they're still going to want to eat meals — which are our games. There is no substitute for the live game experience. We believe that greater fan engagement through social media helps drive television ratings. We have built an enormous global social media community. We estimate roughly 1.4 billion people are connecting with the NBA in some way."[4]

Indeed, Gen Z, and soon Gen Alpha, live through their social media. For them, it's not just a side interest like newspapers or radio were to their grandparents, it is a minute by minute part of their day. It is how they connect with local friends that they see in school but also peers throughout their country and world. But individuals, not teams or leagues, fascinate them.

Cristiano Ronaldo, the global soccer star, currently playing for the Italian club Juventus, has almost half a billion people following across his Instagram, Facebook and Twitter accounts. That's three times more than his club and league combined. LeBron James, the basketball star of the Los Angeles Lakers, also has three times as many followers on his social media than his team and 20 million more than his league. Online fantasy sports, picking individual players to be on a virtual team, grew wildly popular with Millennials and Gen Y and is now into its third generation almost as a standalone entity.

Nielsen, the global ratings and research company, also notes that while Gen Z live on their phones, they are not couch potatoes either. But, like their entertainment, they like their sports to be fast-paced. In a survey of Gen Z in China, France, Germany, Italy, Japan, Spain, the UK and the US, they found that basketball and soccer were the dominant favorites to play among team sports, with surfing, mixed martial arts and extreme sports also popular. Compared to adults over the age of 25, Gen Z were less interested in slower or monotonous sports like baseball, golf and motor sports.[5]

Then there's Playstation and Xbox. While their parents played video games, Gen Z and, soon, Gen Alpha have fused their love of technology, social interaction and fast-paced entertainment with the popular gaming platforms, either on the big screen TV or on their phones. Just like on social media, they connect with people through gaming that they will probably never meet in person. And they are doing it together in numbers that dwarf the traditional outlets of movies, music and TV.

According to an industry report from Newzoo,[6] total worldwide viewership, not playing but just watching, of competitive e-sports will take another leap to 550 million in 2021, a 64% increase from the already large 2017 audience of 335 million.

"For this reason, we also call them Generation Glass because the glass that they interact on now and will wear on their wrist, as glasses on their face, that will be on the Head Up Display of the driverless car they are transported in, or the interactive school desk where they learn will transform how they work, shop, learn, connect and play[7]," said McCrindle.

Training in the Real World

The best environment to learn playmaker decision skills is on the field, court or ice, just as the most efficient learning activity is playing the sport. Surrounded by the constraints and dealing with their personal traits teaches young athletes the nuances of decision-making through raw repetition. Building that tacit knowledge with thousands of slightly distinct patterns of play is the fuel for choosing wisely in the next game. Technology, analytics or passive observation will not replace receiving structured, specific feedback from an experienced coach. Being in the center of the action, making the calls and reacting to changing conditions tests the playmaker like no other environment.

K. Anders Ericsson, the late, well-respected psychology professor at Florida State University, believed that certain positions on the field lend themselves to being a playmaker by their geographically strategic location. Before his untimely passing in 2020, we discussed with him the playmaker role, especially in a decision-making context.

"In most teams, there's some organization where you actually have a structure. It's a little bit like in surgical teams. There's the surgeon who basically would take input from other people, but he or she is sort of the major decision maker. If it really comes to a critical phase, they are more or less taking over, and also may be held responsible for the outcome.

I would argue that in basketball or soccer there are certain types of positions that are localized in such a way that the person who has that playmaking role would basically be located in a way that would have maximal options available to him. Whereas if you penetrate too much, then the number of options that you can actually consider at a single time is going to be much more restricted than somebody who is playing closer to their offensive zone and basically can observe the movements of all the various players. Basically, that's what I would associate with being a playmaker. I'm fine with everyone being playmakers, but at least in the teams that I've looked at, you really do have kind of an assignment of being a playmaker. It's a little bit of a hierarchical structure where some individuals seem to be given the opportunities here of making more of the decisions for the players on the team.[8]"

And playmakers in those advantageous positions gather and store the patterns and representations that produce a lattice framework from which they can pull from memory in a similar situation. This learning cycle must repeat itself, whether that is measured in a number of hours (say, 10,000), or in the number of game-like exposures, to mold the playmaker's inventory of options.

"I think, from all my discussions with athletes, the really good athletes have those representations where they see options and then they basically are making efforts to realize a particular option," Ericsson told us. "They can also diagnose afterwards, if they were unsuccessful, what the source of the problem is and then ideally finding practice conditions that would be able to increase their control over their execution such that they would be able to realize the goal much more reliably in the future."[9]

While a real training environment is ideal, its use is not unlimited. Kids have school, families, friends and other activities that fill their schedules. Physical fatigue alone prevents practicing their sport beyond a few hours each day. Mental burnout is regularly cited among teens as their primary reason for quitting a sport. But what if there was a supplemental learning ecosystem that kids already love — a place where Gen Z and Gen Alpha could engage with their friends, be mentally challenged, and just have fun? Tired from a day of school, two hours of sport training and a load of homework, if only they could "relax" with an activity that they considered a reward for a tough day. Shawn Green has an idea.

Just Don't Tell Them It's Good For Their Brain

"Action games are associated with improvements on a pretty broad range of perceptual and cognitive skills," says Green, an associate professor of psychology at the University of Wisconsin-Madison who specializes in the rate, depth and transfer of learning.[10]

In his aptly named Learning and Transfer lab on the fourth floor of the austere Brogdon Psychology Building, Green and his team of graduate researchers play a lot of video games. But not just any video game and not just for pure enjoyment. Starting with his own graduate research as part of Dr. Daphne Bavelier's lab at the University of Rochester, Green continues to add documented evidence that playing first or third person "shooter" games is the key to producing lasting changes to our brain.

Think of wildly popular games like Call of Duty, Counter Strike or Overwatch requiring the user to outsmart, evade or shoot the bad guys from a "through your eyes" point of view. While the violence of these games has received a bad rap from some parents, the intensity of the visual and audio scenes drives a gamer to give 100 percent cognitive focus to every second. It is this exhilaration that seems to be the difference maker when compared to other so-called "brain training" games.

In fact, a 2015 study[11] asked a group of college undergraduate volunteers to play the action game Portal 2 for eight hours while another group of students played Lumosity, the leading brain-training game. In just that short time, the Portal 2 players showed significant improvements in problem-solving, spatial skills and persistence tests compared to their earlier baselines, while the Lumosity group showed no gains.

"I was really just entranced by [Portal 2]," said Dr. Val Shute, professor of education at Florida State University and lead author of the study. "While I was playing it, I was thinking, I'm really engaging in all sorts of problem-solving."[12]

Commenting on the study, Dr. Green added, "If entertainment games actually do a better job than games designed for neuroplasticity, what that suggests is that we are clearly missing something important about neuroplasticity." It is neuroplasticity, the brain's ability to adapt both physically and functionally to new stimuli, that helps us learn new skills over time. Green wonders if the apps specifically touted to improve our brain actually have met their match. "Have we actually found the active ingredients for neuroplasticity, or are these commercial games sort of better?"[13]

From her Brain and Learning lab at the University of Geneva in Switzerland, Dr. Bavelier tells the story of how Green, her former graduate student, stumbled onto the insight that has driven both of their research tracks for the last two decades.

"When I moved to Rochester, we were investigating the concept of 'useful fields of view' – the visual area over which information can be extracted at a brief glance and which generally decreases with aging. We were looking at whether this function may be altered in deaf individuals since previous research documented enhanced peripheral visual attention following early onset deafness. For this project, a young undergraduate lab tech, Shawn Green, programmed a version of the useful field of view task.

Surprisingly, when Shawn piloted the study on himself and a few other students, all the subjects scored near 100%–

much better than what was expected based on previous studies! These were clearly outliers from the normal population. When we looked for commonalities between the pilot subjects, we found that all of them belonged to an action video game club. Considering the large effect, we changed the project from studying deafness to studying the effect of video games. A short time later, Shawn, who is now on the faculty at the University of Wisconsin, and I authored a *Nature* paper[14] showing that action video games improved attention. We really took something that was unexpected and ran with it!"

In her 2012 TED Talk, Dr. Bavelier revealed that the areas of the brain active in allocating attention change in action video gamers. "So in the same way that we actually see the effects of video games on people's behavior, we can use brain imaging and look at the impact of video games on the brain, and we do find many changes, but the main changes are actually to the brain networks that control attention. So one part is the parietal cortex, which is very well known to control the orientation of attention. The other one is the frontal lobe, which controls how we sustain attention, and another one is the anterior cingulate, which controls how we allocate and regulate attention and resolve conflict. Now, when we do brain imaging, we find that all three of these networks are actually much more efficient in people that play action games."

And just like not all food is good for you and consumed

in moderation, Dr. Bavelier recommends that action video games can provide cognitive benefits when balanced with sleep, social interaction, homework and exercise. "Action video games have a number of ingredients that are actually really powerful for brain plasticity, learning, attention, vision, etc., and so we need and we're working on understanding what are those active ingredients so that we can really then leverage them to deliver better games."[15]

In the years since her talk, Dr. Bavelier has continued her research partnership with Dr. Green to extend our understanding of how these games can help young playmakers, both in their sport and in their schoolwork. An update they wrote in a 2016 Scientific American feature article detailed their experimental process to show not only that existing gamers have superior cognitive skills to non-gamers but how to grow the abilities of a test group by playing the games, then measuring the effect over time.

"To be able to make a clear statement about the effects of these games, we had to provide a firm demonstration that the benefits of action video games are genuine—and that playing these games actually causes players' superior concentration and quick reaction times. After all, it may be that these games simply attract players with exceptional attention—which, in turn, leads to stellar performance on both games and subsequent tests assessing players' cognitive functioning. To show a true cause-and-effect relation, scientists recruit a group of individuals who rarely play video games.

After undergoing a pretest of cognitive skills, this larger group is randomly split into two. One group plays an action game, whereas a control group immerses itself in a social game or another non-action game. Each group is required to play about one hour a day, five days a week for a period of several weeks. A few days after this sustained training, participants are again tested on the same psychological tests they took before playing the games. Groups trained on action games show consistently larger gains in cognition than control groups."[16]

Now, blasting Zombies for hours while sitting on the basement couch does not necessarily describe an ideal brain enhancement strategy for most kids. But, for tomorrow's playmakers, playing a first or third person (looking over the shoulder of your hero) sports game may serve a dual purpose - exercising their visual attention, memory, decision-making and reaction time while picking up the subtle cues of rules and tactics of their sport in a time-pressured, emotional and rewarding game.

Professional soccer players spend hours off the field playing EA Sports' FIFA game on their Xbox, PlayStation or phone. NFL stars spend their idle time with the latest Madden football game. But even more interesting is that many pro and college athletes crossover to play a different sport virtually; basketball players on FIFA or hockey players on NBA 2K.

And now there is a new generation of sport-specific virtual training environments, like Sense Arena[17] for hockey and gameSense Sports[18] for baseball. The energy and motivation to play and beat friends fires the same learning areas of the brain as the real thing, without the physical fatigue, or the "chocolate" of the learning process, as Dr. Bavelier dubs it.

"There are brain scientists like me that are beginning to understand what are the good ingredients in games to promote positive effects, and that's what I'm going to call the broccoli side of the equation. There is an entertainment software industry which is extremely deft at coming up with appealing products that you can't resist. That's the chocolate side of the equation. The issue is we need to put the two together, and it's a little bit like with food. Who really wants to eat chocolate-covered broccoli?

And you probably have had that feeling, picking up an education game and sort of feeling, hmm, you know, it's not really fun, it's not really engaging. So what we need is really a new brand of chocolate, a brand of chocolate that is irresistible, that you really want to play, but that has all the ingredients, the good ingredients that are extracted from the broccoli that you can't recognize but are still working on your brains."[19]

So, as parents and coaches, we may think studying their playbooks or watching real athletes play the game is the best use of our players' downtime, but don't underestimate the power of fun they get from the sophisticated design of sports video games. Maybe include it in your recommended at-home training for a few hours per week, after they finish their homework and chores and before bedtime. As an extra reward, they can then go kill some zombies.

The Tao of Carletto

The question didn't surprise Paul Clement, unlike the players seated in front of him. On the eve of the 2010 FA Cup final, England's most prestigious soccer tournament, the Chelsea FC team gathered to hear the tactical game plan from the coaching staff. A week before, they had secured the Premier League title and were poised to achieve the club's first league and cup double.

As Clement stood at a blank sheet of flip-chart paper with black marker in hand, he watched the players' faces as their manager, Carlo Ancelotti, asked them a simple question.

"This is the last game of the season. We know what we're able to do and we know the opposition. What do you think the tactics should be?"

At first, Clement recalled the blank stares, even from the senior players, including club legends like Frank Lampard, John Terry, and Petr Cech. Once they realized this was not a rhetorical question, the ideas flowed. "I scribbled notes down as fast as I could and, before you knew it, we had a list of defending points and a list of attacking ones," said Clement, who had become Ancelotti's assistant coach.

With the tactics settled, the Blues beat Portsmouth the next day, 1-0, in front of over 90,000 fans at England's Wembley Stadium, to lift the historic FA Cup trophy.

"Sometimes coaches are scared to give that responsibility to the players," said Clement. "But ultimately that's what it's all about. When a game goes on, how much can a coach influence what's happening, when you can't get information across to the players? They need to be able to make those decisions in split-second moments. The more responsibility the players take, the better."

Clement credits Ancelotti with teaching him the human side of coaching. After becoming his right-hand man at Chelsea, Clement followed Ancelotti on a grand tour of the world's great soccer clubs, Paris Saint-Germain, Real Madrid and Bayern Munich. Prior to his arrival at Chelsea in 2009, Ancelotti had already won the UEFA Champions League twice at AC Milan.

In 2014, he would win it again, with Clement at his side at Real Madrid. At each stop, the relationships that Ancelotti built meant the most to building a successful team, according to Clement, "I'm sometimes asked whether there are any non-negotiables with Carlo and it's a hard question: he builds such strong relationships with people that almost everything feels like it's negotiable. He has such a fantastic relationship with the players, built on total respect. He puts himself on the same level as them, wanting feedback from them and wanting to help them and guide them."[20]

As Ancelotti himself explains, "I have managed

superstars — Cristiano Ronaldo, Zlatan Ibrahimovic — but they are superstars outside the training ground. The atmosphere outside builds the superstar. In the dressing room, they are exactly the same. At the end, I have to manage people, not players. They are not players: They are people who play football. I am not a manager. I am a man that works as a manager. I think this is an important point."[21]

And when the players believe their coach cares for and listens to them, the conversation can turn to the best approach to beat an opponent. With their buy-in that they helped develop the game's tactics, players make more coherent in-game decisions. This superior decision-making is, truly, the playmaker's advantage as Ancelotti has witnessed through the years.

"The clearest example of decision-making in my industry can be seen on the pitch. I am always impressed by the manner in which the top players are differentiated from the rest primarily by their decision-making and its effect upon the team," writes Ancelotti. "Take the true greats – the likes of Maradona, Pelé, Cruyff. If you were to watch a film of them playing and pause it just before they made their pass, you could ask a hundred coaches where they should play the ball and they would all say the same thing: 'It should go there.' When you press play, the film will show the ball going exactly there. Great players invariably play that 'correct' ball – they make the right decision. Naturally, everybody wants to score, but if somebody else is in a better position, they make the right decision to pass. It's these decisions that, over the course of a match, decide who wins and loses.

Players have to make these decisions in an instant; examples from today's game are (Cristiano) Ronaldo and (Zlatan) Ibrahimović. Players like Ibra will always make the right decision for the team, not only in the game but also in training. Many say that it is nature, not nurture, that gives these players this ability–but we know it can be trained. When I trained Cristiano at Madrid, he already had this ability, but if you look at him in his early days at Manchester United you see a different, more selfish player at the start. Sir Alex (Ferguson) and his staff trained him to be a team player. That's the difference between an engaged player (who is fully committed) and an aligned player (whose "commitment always works for the greater good of the team). You need them to be both."[22]

And while many coaches focus on their best players, Ancelotti has always supported the youth academies at his clubs, learning the names of dozens of developing prospects while mixing in with them at their training sessions. Building their confidence and teaching them how to use their talents within a system of play should be the coach's priority.

"With young players it is a little bit different. For the young players you have to do some specific work to improve their limits, to improve their understanding of the game and their role within different systems, and also some technical work in areas where they might be deficient. So, with the eighteen-year-old Ronaldo who signed for Manchester United, it was important that he understood the team dynamics, and within the United system his crossing and decision-making needed work. Sir Alex and his coaches at Manchester would only have been concerned with his technique where it was applied towards the needs of the team. By the time he was at Madrid, it had become a case of working out how we could best get the team to extract the most value from his talent. So, the development needs gradually change as the player grows.

Great players are great decision-makers. They know when to pass, when to shoot, when to defend, when to attack, all for the most benefit to the team. The manager of a very talented player has to convince the player to put this talent to the service of the team–this is how they can continue to develop"

"I have to find a way to keep this talent alive and efficient, but to deploy it within the system of the team. I don't want them to sacrifice their unique quality – they have to keep that – and, equally, I have to make the team understand the special value that such players can add."[23]

Ownership, Autonomy and Responsibility

Ancelotti's philosophy transcends soccer, transferring to all sports. Understanding each player first, not just their specific, athletic skills but their hopes, fears, strengths and insecurities, will paint a picture of why that player makes certain decisions and how they can contribute to the entire team. By granting players ownership, autonomy and responsibility of their decisions, they will be more adaptable to the wide variety of game situations they will face.

While it is excruciatingly frustrating for coaches (and parents) to allow poor decisions in the short term, the trial-and-error process will produce more malleable minds in the long run. The coach should take on the role of a facilitator who creates game-like scenarios and then asks questions when there is a break in play. Rather than cynical, sarcastic questions ("Why would you pass to her there?), ask questions that probe the decision-making process ("What did you see right before you made that pass?)

Specifically, here is an eight point checklist, from the experts at UK Coaching,[24] for building stronger decision makers:

1. Allow freedom: Involve players by empowering them to develop creative training activities.
2. Mix it up: Create training sessions that put players in unfamiliar situations so they have to develop solutions to the problems posed.
3. No more cones: Create situations where players have to negotiate the actions of opponents. Rather than using static markers use players who move around to create continually changing

situations that require a range of decisions to be made.

4. Ask questions: Encourage players to question each other and provide feedback on their performance.

5. Keep it positive: Encourage deliberate practice with positive feedback. Apply four times the amount of praise to criticism and use positive reinforcement to challenge players.

6. Seek variety: Maximize players' exposure to as many playing situations as possible. Constant reinforcement of playing scenarios improves intuitive decision-making.

7. Build memory: Avoid too much structure with younger players and encourage them with deliberate play in a wide range of activities to improve pattern recall and recognition in later stages of development (pattern recall and recognition is the ability of a player to access information stored in memory and then reconstruct in response to a given event).

8. Recommend different but related sports: Playing sports of a similar type will develop core sports skills and will enhance all-round decision-making ability.

In his four years at UCLA, Kareem Abdul-Jabbar raised three national championship trophies under the leadership of John Wooden, considered by many to be the most effective coach ever, in any sport. In his 2017 bestselling book, "Coach Wooden and Me", he chronicled the bits and pieces of Wooden's coaching habits and style. Beyond the well-known tidbits of learning to put on your socks and shoes correctly, Abdul-Jabbar dove deeper into the motivations behind his beloved college coach.

"Practices were highly structured, scheduled to the minute, to the second, to the nanosecond. We knew that he spent two hours every morning just working out the schedule for that day's two-hour practice. He wrote everything down on three-by-five-inch index cards and kept a loose-leaf notebook with detailed notes of every practice session. Most other coaches would simply have pulled out their familiar list of drills that they used every year with every team.

But Coach's philosophy was that teams were much more fluid. Other coaches saw their teams as a deck of cards. If one card dropped off, they just grabbed another card from the deck. The cards were interchangeable because they only looked at the backs of the cards. Coach Wooden looked at the face value of each card. No two cards were alike, just as no two players were alike. Even more interesting, he realized that a particular player was not the same player one day that he had been the day before, that each time one player progressed or faltered, the whole team's ability to read one another and predict what each would do was affected.[25]"

As with most successful tactical plans, the UCLA offense was fluid, allowing the players to respond to what opportunities presented themselves, according to Abdul-Jabbar.

"After we did our drills, we scrimmaged. During a game, what often appeared to be spontaneous on the court was actually the result of hours of practicing until our responses finally became spontaneous and instantaneous. We didn't have any set plays. We had a basic offensive system—you go here, you go there, you go in that corner, stand over there—and then we would run several options off it, depending on how our opponents defended us. Our offense was structured to recognize opportunities as a group and take advantage of them."

The Future is Decisive

So, we have come full circle, all the way around the Athlete Decision Model. Traits that differentiate each athlete, Attention, Cognition and Emotion, constrained by Time, Rules and Tactics. Understanding how these common challenges affect individuals differently is the secret sauce of developing playmakers. Installing a measurement system for the hundreds of player decisions in a game requires some creative common sense about what we are trying to improve. Finally, giving players the space and freedom to learn, at practices and in games, builds their tacit knowledge library of patterns and rules that they can borrow from throughout their playing careers.

Athlete Decision Model™

NOTES

Introduction

1. https://www.usatoday.com/story/sports/ncaaf/sec/2017/07/12/nick-saban-alabama-sec-media-days/471639001/
2. https://medium.com/thrive-global/heres-the-mindset-of-elite-athletes-53c6ecd5e3a6
3. https://geni.us/ThePlaymakersAdvantage
4. https://www.nflpenalties.com/all-penalties.php?&year=2019
5. https://nesn.com/2017/01/bill-belichicks-do-your-job-mantra-goes-way-back-as-this-2000-interview-shows/

1. Attention

1. https://www.youtube.com/watch?v=_gHpcmj82qg
2. https://www.baltimoreravens.com/news/peyton-manning-ed-reed-is-nfl-s-best-safety-9084800
3. https://www.youtube.com/watch?v=_gHpcmj82qg
4. https://sports.yahoo.com/news/simply-put--there-was-no-one-like-greg-maddux-212210058.html
5. https://www.mlb.com/news/former-braves-catcher-eddie-perez-reflects-on-greg-madduxs-greatness/c-66355592
6. https://www.mlb.com/news/former-braves-catcher-eddie-perez-reflects-on-greg-madduxs-greatness/c-66355592
7. https://www.baseball-almanac.com/quotes/greg_maddux_quotes.shtml
8. https://vault.si.com/vault/1995/08/14/once-in-a-lifetime-greg-maddux-of-the-braves-is-the-best-righthander-in-the-past-75-yearsbut-he-would-rather-you-didnt-know-it
9. https://www.si.com/more-sports/2008/08/27/greg-maddux

10. https://theathletic.com/1631137/2020/02/25/the-baseball-100-no-31-greg-maddux/

11. https://www.smithsonianmag.com/arts-culture/teller-reveals-his-secrets-100744801/

12. https://www.nature.com/articles/nrn2473

13. http://macknik.neuralcorrelate.com/pdf/articles/sciam08.pdf

14. https://www.frontiersin.org/articles/10.3389/fnhum.2011.00133/full

15. http://www.chabris.com/Simons1999.pdf

16. https://youtu.be/IGQmdoK_ZfY

17. https://www.nature.com/articles/nrn2473

18. https://peerj.com/articles/19/

19. https://youtu.be/2QwdzuqwzW4

20. http://macknik.neuralcorrelate.com/pdf/articles/sciammind2010.pdf

21. https://www.nature.com/articles/nrn2473

22. https://www.goal.com/en/news/too-many-stepovers-alex-ferguson-cristiano-ronaldo/1rezmo5ndajss1ie9m4p8nbvnp

23. https://www.frontiersin.org/articles/10.3389/fpsyg.2018.02043/full

24. https://doi.org/10.1123/jsep.35.1.98

25. https://doi.org/10.1123/jsep.35.1.98

26. https://www.brunel.ac.uk/news-and-events/news/articles/Footballers-are-better-at-predicting-opponents-movements-MRI-research-finds

27. https://www.thesun.co.uk/sport/football/169264/paolo-maldini-the-defender-so-good-he-didnt-even-need-to-tackle/

28. https://www.thesun.co.uk/archives/football/169264/paolo-maldini-the-defender-so-good-he-didnt-even-need-to-tackle/

29. https://www.nytimes.com/2016/11/22/sports/tennis/deaf-player-lee-duck-hee-south-korea.html

30. https://www.nytimes.com/2016/11/22/sports/tennis/deaf-player-lee-duck-hee-south-korea.html

31. https://www.ncbi.nlm.nih.gov/pmc/articles/PMC4456887/

32. https://www.nytimes.com/2016/11/22/sports/tennis/deaf-player-lee-duck-hee-south-korea.html

33. https://www.atptour.com/en/news/star-of-tomorrow-2015-duckhee-lee

34. https://www.atptour.com/en/news/star-of-tomorrow-2015-duckhee-lee

35. https://uk.reuters.com/article/uk-tennis-wimbledon-grunting-sb/game-set-and-grunt-wimbledon-faces-noise-pollution-idUKTRE55L0E520090622

36. https://www.tennisworldusa.org/tennis/news/Maria_Sharapova/78644/maria-sharapova-my-throat-hurts-after-every-match-because-of-grunting-/

37. https://www.uni-jena.de/en/190502_tennis_grunting.html

38. https://www.nytimes.com/2014/11/23/sports/packers-aaron-rodgers-has-a-voice-that-leaves-defenders-muttering.html

39. https://operations.nfl.com/stats-central/stats-articles/aaron-rodgers-takes-advantage-of-free-plays-better-than-anyone/

40. https://www.si.com/nfl/seahawks/news/seahawks-game-planning-for-aaron-rodgers-hard-count-mastery

41. https://www.nytimes.com/2014/11/23/sports/packers-aaron-rodgers-has-a-voice-that-leaves-defenders-muttering.html

2. Cognition

1. https://www.si.com/nba/lakers/news/inside-the-mind-of-lebron-james-a-look-at-his-iq

2. https://youtu.be/tUEQr_8URz8

3. https://www.espn.com/nba/story/_/id/11067098/lebron-james-greatest-weapon-brain

4. https://www.espn.com/nba/story/_/id/11067098/lebron-james-greatest-weapon-brain

5. https://www.si.com/nba/lakers/news/inside-the-mind-of-lebron-james-a-look-at-his-iq

6. https://www.si.com/nba/lakers/news/inside-the-mind-of-lebron-james-a-look-at-his-iq

7. My Book

8. https://www.espn.com/nfl/story/_/id/17546974/nfl-photographic-memory-green-bay-packers-qb-aaron-rodgers

9. https://www.espn.com/nfl/story/_/id/17546974/nfl-photographic-memory-green-bay-packers-qb-aaron-rodgers

10. Knopik, V. S., Neiderhiser, J. M., DeFries, J. C., & Plomin, R. (2016). Behavioral genetics
    (7th edn). New York: Macmillan Higher Education.
11. Voss, Michelle W., Arthur F. Kramer, Chandramallika Basak, Ruchika Shaurya Prakash, and Brent Roberts, "Are Expert Athletes 'Expert' in the Cognitive Laboratory? A Meta-Analytic Review of Cognition and Sport Expertise," Applied Cognitive Psychology 24 (6) 2009: 812–26.
12. https://doi.org/10.1002/acp.3526
13. Biermann, Christoph. Football Hackers (p. 246). 2019 Blink Publishing. Kindle Edition.
14. Biermann, Christoph. Football Hackers (p. 246). 2019 Blink Publishing. Kindle Edition.
15. http://causeriesfoot.com/2020/04/05/de-la-tete-aux-pieds/
16. https://www.skysports.com/football/story-telling/11095/12003088/why-tsg-hoffenheim-are-footballs-most-innovative-club
17. https://www.skysports.com/football/story-telling/11095/12003088/why-tsg-hoffenheim-are-footballs-most-innovative-club
18. https://www.skysports.com/football/story-telling/11095/12003088/why-tsg-hoffenheim-are-footballs-most-innovative-club
19. https://www.frontiersin.org/articles/10.3389/fpsyg.2019.02773/full
20. https://www.frontiersin.org/articles/10.3389/fpsyg.2019.02773/full
21. https://www.frontiersin.org/articles/10.3389/fpsyg.2019.02773/full
22. https://www.frontiersin.org/articles/10.3389/fpsyg.2019.02773/full
23. www.dst.defence.gov.au/news/2017/01/04/dst-driving-cognitive-performance-research
24. https://issuu.com/faircountmediaasia-pacific/docs/defence_science_and_technology_outl/134
25. https://www.frontiersin.org/articles/10.3389/fnhum.2019.00466/full

3. Emotion

1. https://www.youtube.com/watch?v=vqOjKuiMQ20
2. https://sports.yahoo.com/alabamas-mekhi-brown-sideline-meltdown-something-stupid-cost-us-game-081410660.html
3. ANXIETY, STRESS, & COPING, Routledge, 2019, https://doi.org/10.1080/10615806.2019.1643459.

4. Anticipation and Decision Making in Sport (p. 234). Taylor and Francis. 2019

5. ANXIETY, STRESS, & COPING, Routledge, 2019, https://doi.org/10.1080/10615806.2019.1643459.

6. ANXIETY, STRESS, & COPING, Routledge, 2019, https://doi.org/10.1080/10615806.2019.1643459.

7. ANXIETY, STRESS, & COPING, Routledge, 2019, https://doi.org/10.1080/10615806.2019.1643459.

8. https://www.nbcsports.com/philadelphia/eagles/blunt-assessment-jim-schwartz-eagles-cornerbacks-sidney-jones-rasul-douglas

9. https://econpapers.repec.org/RePEc:sae:jospec:v:12:y:2011:i:3:p:231-252

10. Front. Psychol., 30 April 2019 | https://doi.org/10.3389/fpsyg.2019.00919

11. https://www.nbc.com/running-wild-with-bear-grylls/video/roger-federer/3755843

12. https://www.nytimes.com/2009/09/10/sports/tennis/10federer.html

13. https://www.nytimes.com/2009/09/10/sports/tennis/10federer.html

14. https://www.nbc.com/running-wild-with-bear-grylls/video/roger-federer/3755843

15. https://www.express.co.uk/sport/tennis/871764/Roger-Federer-quotes

16. http://dx.doi.org/10.1080/02699931.2015.1044424

17. https://doi.org/10.1080/02699931.2018.1464434

18. http://eprints.chi.ac.uk/id/eprint/3272/1/RunswicketalPsychologicalResearch-AcceptedVersion.pdf

19. https://www.sbnation.com/nba/2019/5/6/18531275/kawhi-leonard-quotes-toronto-raptors-interview

20. https://www.si.com/nba/2016/03/14/kawhi-leonard-spurs-tim-duncan-gregg-popovich-tony-parker-manu-ginobili

21. https://www.si.com/nba/2016/03/14/kawhi-leonard-spurs-tim-duncan-gregg-popovich-tony-parker-manu-ginobili

22. https://www.sbnation.com/nba/2019/5/6/18531275/kawhi-leonard-quotes-toronto-raptors-interview

23. https://dailystoic.com/Epictetus/

24. https://www.si.com/nfl/2015/12/08/ryan-holiday-nfl-stoicism-book-pete-carroll-bill-belichick
25. https://www.si.com/nfl/2015/12/08/ryan-holiday-nfl-stoicism-book-pete-carroll-bill-belichick
26. https://www.blazersedge.com/2018/4/10/17220370/emotionless-mccollum-not-worried-about-slump-jason-quick
27. https://www.espn.com/blog/san-antonio-spurs/post/_/id/1090/kawhi-leonard-hits-milestone-in-spurs-win-over-pelicans
28. https://www.si.com/nba/2016/03/14/kawhi-leonard-spurs-tim-duncan-gregg-popovich-tony-parker-manu-ginobili
29. https://www.imdb.com/title/tt1612105/
30. https://www.imdb.com/title/tt1612105/
31. https://www.theguardian.com/sport/blog/2018/sep/24/tiger-woods-earl-pga-tour
32. Unprecendented: The Masters and Me, Tiger Woods and Lorne Rubenstein, 2017, Sphere
33. Holiday, Ryan. Stillness Is the Key (p. 88). Penguin Publishing Group. Kindle Edition.
34. Kegelaers, J., Wylleman, P., & Oudejans, R. R. D. (2020). A coach perspective on the use of planned
    disruptions in high-performance sports. Sport, Exercise, and Performance Psychology, 9(1), 29-44.
    https://doi.org/10.1037/spy0000167
35. Kegelaers, J., Wylleman, P., & Oudejans, R. R. D. (2020). A coach perspective on the use of planned
    disruptions in high-performance sports. Sport, Exercise, and Performance Psychology, 9(1), 29-44.
    https://doi.org/10.1037/spy0000167
36. Kegelaers, J., Wylleman, P., & Oudejans, R. R. D. (2020). A coach perspective on the use of planned
    disruptions in high-performance sports. Sport, Exercise, and Performance Psychology, 9(1), 29-44.
    https://doi.org/10.1037/spy0000167
37. Kegelaers, J., Wylleman, P., & Oudejans, R. R. D. (2020). A coach perspective on the use of planned
    disruptions in high-performance sports. Sport, Exercise, and Performance Psychology, 9(1), 29-44.

https://doi.org/10.1037/spy0000167

38. https://www.espn.com/espn/story/_/id/29200293/the-ancient-credo-fueled-patriot-way-inspired-nick-saban-helped-ryan-shazier-heal

4. Time

1. Coram, R. (2002). Boyd: The Fighter Pilot Who Changed the Art of War. United States: Little, Brown.
2. Coram, R. (2002). Boyd: The Fighter Pilot Who Changed the Art of War. United States: Little, Brown.
3. Coram, R. (2002). Boyd: The Fighter Pilot Who Changed the Art of War. United States: Little, Brown.
4. The Mind of War: John Boyd and American Security; Grant Hammond, 2012, Smithsonian Institution; 1588343642
5. https://www.businessinsider.com/steph-curry-interview-on-basketball-life-championships-2016-2
6. https://www.thecut.com/2016/06/steph-curry-perception-performance.html
7. https://web.archive.org/web/20061024220205/http://www.codeonemagazine.com/archives/1997/articles/jul_97/jul2_97_p.html
8. https://web.archive.org/web/20061024220205/http://www.codeonemagazine.com/archives/1997/articles/jul_97/jul2_97_p.html
9. https://fasttransients.files.wordpress.com/2010/03/patternsofconflict1.pdf
10. https://www.marca.com/en/football/real-madrid/2018/12/03/5c05b1b3e2704e01978b45ab.html
11. https://goldenfoot.com/
12. https://www.skysports.com/football/news/11835/10842948/luka-modric-is-still-key-for-real-madrid-under-zinedine-zidane
13. https://www.skysports.com/football/news/11835/10842948/luka-modric-is-still-key-for-real-madrid-under-zinedine-zidane
14. https://www.marca.com/en/football/real-madrid/2018/12/04/5c065514e2704e2a178b4599.html
15. https://www.worldsoccer.com/features/luka-modric-396393

16. https://www.worldsoccer.com/features/luka-modric-396393
17. Author interview with Gary Klein
18. Klein, Gary, "Naturalistic Decision Making," Human Factors: The Journal of the Human Factors and Ergonomics Society 50 (3) 2008: 456–60.
19. Author interview with Gary Klein
20. Gary A. Klein, (1998) "Sources of Power: How People Make Decisions", MIT Press, Cambridge, Mass
21. https://www.realmadrid.com/en/news/2019/12/12/modric-an-expert-at-scoring-from-outside-the-box
22. Gary A. Klein, (1998) "Sources of Power: How People Make Decisions", MIT Press, Cambridge, Mass
23. Gary A. Klein, (1998) "Sources of Power: How People Make Decisions", MIT Press, Cambridge, Mass
24. Gary A. Klein, (1998) "Sources of Power: How People Make Decisions", MIT Press, Cambridge, Mass
25. Author interview with Gary Klein
26. Gary A. Klein, (1998) "Sources of Power: How People Make Decisions", MIT Press, Cambridge, Mass
27. Author interview with Gary Klein

5. Rules

1. https://twitter.com/TomBrady/status/1174850764839276544?s=20
2. https://twitter.com/TomBrady/status/1174852537368948736
3. https://operations.nfl.com/the-rules/2019-rules-changes-and-points-of-emphasis/
4. https://www.foxsports.com/nfl/video/1607072323988
5. https://dfkoz.tumblr.com/post/26772798385/the-most-complicated-sport-in-the-world
6. https://fivethirtyeight.com/features/how-much-football-is-even-in-a-football-broadcast/
7. https://www.basketball-reference.com/leagues/NBA_stats_per_game.html
8. https://www.hockey-reference.com/leagues/NHL_2019.html

9. https://www.whoscored.com/Regions/252/Tournaments/2/Seasons/4311/Stages/9155/TeamStatistics/England-Premier-League-2014-2015

10. https://www.lexico.com/en/definition/rule

11. https://www.lexico.com/en/definition/fair

12. https://www.lexico.com/en/definition/sport

13. https://operations.nfl.com/the-rules/evolution-of-the-nfl-rules/

14. https://www.sbnation.com/2018/9/23/17893402/clay-matthews-nfl-roughing-the-passer-rule-packers

15. https://www.sbnation.com/2018/9/23/17893402/clay-matthews-nfl-roughing-the-passer-rule-packers

16. https://operations.nfl.com/the-rules/2019-nfl-rulebook/#article-11.-roughing-the-passer

17. MacMahon, Clare & Mildenhall, Bill. (2012). A Practical Perspective on Decision Making Influences in Sports Officiating. International Journal of Sports Science and Coaching. 7. 153-166. 10.1260/1747-9541.7.1.153.

18. MacMahon, Clare & Mildenhall, Bill. (2012). A Practical Perspective on Decision Making Influences in Sports Officiating. International Journal of Sports Science and Coaching. 7. 153-166. 10.1260/1747-9541.7.1.153.

19. MacMahon, Clare & Mildenhall, Bill. (2012). A Practical Perspective on Decision Making Influences in Sports Officiating. International Journal of Sports Science and Coaching. 7. 153-166. 10.1260/1747-9541.7.1.153.

20. Plessner, H. and Betsch, T., Sequential Effects in Important Referee Decisions: The Case of Penalties in
   Soccer, Journal of Sport & Exercise Psychology, 2001, 23(3), 254-259.

21. Anderson, K. J., and Pierce, D. A., Officiating Bias: The Effect of Foul Differential on Foul Calls in NCAA
   Basketball, Journal of Sports Sciences, 2009, 27, 687?694.

22. MacMahon, Clare & Mildenhall, Bill. (2012). A Practical Perspective on Decision Making Influences in Sports Officiating. International Journal of Sports Science and Coaching. 7. 153-166. 10.1260/1747-9541.7.1.153.

23. Markus Raab , Simcha Avugos , Michael Bar-Eli & Clare MacMahon

(2020): The referee's challenge: a threshold process model for decision-making in sport games,
International Review of Sport and Exercise Psychology, DOI: 10.1080/1750984X.2020.1783696

24. Helsen, W., & Bultynck, J. B. (2004). Physical and perceptual-cognitive demands of top-class refereeing
in association football. Journal of Sports Sciences, 22(2), 179–189.
https://doi.org/10.1080/02640410310001641502

25. Markus Raab , Simcha Avugos , Michael Bar-Eli & Clare MacMahon
(2020): The referee's challenge: a threshold process model for decision-making in sport games,
International Review of Sport and Exercise Psychology, DOI: 10.1080/1750984X.2020.1783696

26. https://www.mavsmoneyball.com/2020/8/24/21398865/nba-playoffs-2020-dallas-mavericks-quotes-luka-doncic-rick-carlisle

27. https://www.espn.com/nba/story/_/id/29794648/clippers-marcus-morris-fined-35k-mavericks-luka-doncic-15k

28. https://www.espn.com/nba/story/_/id/29774262/la-clippers-marcus-morris-ejected-flagrant-foul-dallas-mavericks-luka-doncic

29. https://www.espn.com/nba/story/_/id/29774262/la-clippers-marcus-morris-ejected-flagrant-foul-dallas-mavericks-luka-doncic

30. https://www.star-telegram.com/sports/nba/dallas-mavericks/article224661695.html

31. *https://www.ocregister.com/2018/10/31/lakers-lebron-james-admires-mavericks-rookie-luka-doncic/*

32. https://twitter.com/BenGolliver/status/1094089979175882752

33. *https://youtu.be/3wPRTJtOh00?t=160*

34. McCarthy, J. F., & Kelly, B. R. (1978a). Aggression, performance variables, and anger self-report in ice hockey players. *Journal of Psychology, 99*, 97-101.

35. Andrews, R. (1974). A Spearman rank order correlation for 18 NHL teams. In *National Hockey League Guide.* Montreal: National Hockey League.

36. Zitek, Emily & Jordan, Alexander. (2011). Anger, Aggression, and Athletics: Technical Fouls Predict Performance Outcomes in the NBA. Athletic Insight. 3. 29-39.

37. Zitek, Emily & Jordan, Alexander. (2011). Anger, Aggression, and Athletics: Technical Fouls Predict Performance Outcomes in the NBA. Athletic Insight. 3. 29-39.

38. Zitek, Emily & Jordan, Alexander. (2011). Anger, Aggression, and Athletics: Technical Fouls Predict Performance Outcomes in the NBA. Athletic Insight. 3. 29-39.

39. Gómez MA, Avugos S, Ortega E et al.
    Adverse effects of technical fouls in
    elite basketball performance.
    Biol Sport. 2019;36(2):155–161.

40. Schild, C., Botzet, L.J., Planert, L., Ścigała, K.A., Zettler, I., Lang, J.W.B., Linking
    Personality Traits to Objective Foul Records in (Semi-)Professional Youth Basketball, Journal of Research in
    Personality (2020), doi: https://doi.org/10.1016/j.jrp.2020.103987

6. Tactics

1. https://www.latimes.com/archives/la-xpm-1987-08-28-sp-2763-story.html

2. https://theathletic.com/1669125/2020/03/16/rene-maric-borussia-monchengladbach/

3. https://www.theguardian.com/football/2018/sep/19/chatroom-bootroom-rene-maric-modern-coach-salzburg

4. https://www.theguardian.com/football/2018/sep/19/chatroom-bootroom-rene-maric-modern-coach-salzburg

5. https://www.spox.com/de/sport/fussball/bundesliga/2003/Artikel/rene-maric-interview-borussia-moenchengladbach-red-bull-salzburg-assistant-manager-coach-english-itw.html

6. https://www.spox.com/de/sport/fussball/bundesliga/2003/Artikel/rene-maric-interview-borussia-moenchengladbach-red-bull-salzburg-assistant-manager-coach-english-itw.html

7. https://theathletic.com/1669125/2020/03/16/rene-maric-borussia-monchengladbach/

8. https://www.spox.com/de/sport/fussball/bundesliga/2003/Artikel/ rene-maric-interview-borussia-moenchengladbach-red-bull-salzburg- assistant-manager-coach-english-itw.html

9. https://www.thetimes.co.uk/edition/sport/real-madrid-will-target- manchester-city-at-the-back-pep-guardiolas-defenders-struggle-to- keep-the-best-teams-out-rhbgnjphj

10. Lex H, Essig K, Knoblauch A, Schack T (2015) Cognitive Representations and Cognitive Processing of Team-Specific Tactics in Soccer. PLoS ONE 10(2): e0118219. https://doi.org/10.1371/ journal.pone.0118219

11. Lex H, Essig K, Knoblauch A, Schack T (2015) Cognitive Representations and Cognitive Processing of Team-Specific Tactics in Soccer. PLoS ONE 10(2): e0118219. https://doi.org/10.1371/ journal.pone.0118219

12. My Book

13. https://www.basketball-reference.com/players/n/nashst01.html

14. https://vault.si.com/vault/2006/01/30/point-guard-from-another- planet

15. Martin, J., & Cox, D. (2016). Positioning Steve Nash: A Theory- Driven, Social Psychological, and Biographical Case Study of Creativity in Sport, The Sport Psychologist, 30(4), 388-398. Retrieved Aug 5, 2020, from https://journals.humankinetics.com/view/ journals/tsp/30/4/article-p388.xml

16. Foran, C. (2005). The world according to Steve Nash. *TORO Magazine.* Retrieved from: http://charlesforan.com/wordpress/ writings-features-the-world-according-to-steve-nash/.

17. Martin, J., & Cox, D. (2016). Positioning Steve Nash: A Theory- Driven, Social Psychological, and Biographical Case Study of Creativity in Sport, The Sport Psychologist, 30(4), 388-398. Retrieved Aug 5, 2020, from https://journals.humankinetics.com/view/ journals/tsp/30/4/article-p388.xml

18. Martin, J., & Cox, D. (2016). Positioning Steve Nash: A Theory- Driven, Social Psychological, and Biographical Case Study of Creativity in Sport, The Sport Psychologist, 30(4), 388-398. Retrieved Aug 5, 2020, from https://journals.humankinetics.com/view/ journals/tsp/30/4/article-p388.xml

19. Martin, J., & Cox, D. (2016). Positioning Steve Nash: A Theory-Driven, Social Psychological, and Biographical Case Study of Creativity in Sport, The Sport Psychologist, 30(4), 388-398. Retrieved Aug 5, 2020, from https://journals.humankinetics.com/view/journals/tsp/30/4/article-p388.xml

20. Martin, J., & Cox, D. (2016). Positioning Steve Nash: A Theory-Driven, Social Psychological, and Biographical Case Study of Creativity in Sport, The Sport Psychologist, 30(4), 388-398. Retrieved Aug 5, 2020, from https://journals.humankinetics.com/view/journals/tsp/30/4/article-p388.xml

21. https://www.theplayerstribune.com/en-us/articles/steve-nash-retirement

22. https://static.nytimes.com/email-content/MSB_5302.html?nlid=82744824

23. https://static.nytimes.com/email-content/MSB_5302.html?nlid=82744824

24. Martin, J., & Cox, D. (2016). Positioning Steve Nash: A Theory-Driven, Social Psychological, and Biographical Case Study of Creativity in Sport, The Sport Psychologist, 30(4), 388-398. Retrieved Aug 5, 2020, from https://journals.humankinetics.com/view/journals/tsp/30/4/article-p388.xml

25. https://www.cbc.ca/films/more/nash

26. https://vault.si.com/vault/2006/01/30/point-guard-from-another-planet

27. https://www.nba.com/video/2018/09/07/20180907-hall-fame-steve-nash-speech

28. https://vault.si.com/vault/2006/01/30/point-guard-from-another-planet

29. https://www.youtube.com/watch?v=jdrS2cyM2Q8

30. Daniel Memmert. 31 Mar 2015 ,Development of Tactical Creativity in Sports from:
    Routledge Handbook of Sport Expertise Routledge.
    Accessed on: 12 Feb 2018
    https://www.routledgehandbooks.com/doi/10.4324/9781315776675.ch31

31. Daniel Memmert. 31 Mar 2015 ,Development of Tactical Creativity in Sports from:

Routledge Handbook of Sport Expertise Routledge.
Accessed on: 12 Feb 2018
https://www.routledgehandbooks.com/doi/10.4324/
9781315776675.ch31

32. Daniel Memmert. 31 Mar 2015 ,Development of Tactical Creativity in Sports from:
Routledge Handbook of Sport Expertise Routledge.
Accessed on: 12 Feb 2018
https://www.routledgehandbooks.-
com/doi/10.4324/9781315776675.ch31

33. Daniel Memmert. 31 Mar 2015 ,Development of Tactical Creativity in Sports from:
Routledge Handbook of Sport Expertise Routledge.
Accessed on: 12 Feb 2018
https://www.routledgehandbooks.-
com/doi/10.4324/9781315776675.ch31

34. Daniel Memmert. 31 Mar 2015 ,Development of Tactical Creativity in Sports from:
Routledge Handbook of Sport Expertise Routledge.
Accessed on: 12 Feb 2018
https://www.routledgehandbooks.-
com/doi/10.4324/9781315776675.ch31

35. Daniel Memmert. 31 Mar 2015 ,Development of Tactical Creativity in Sports from:
Routledge Handbook of Sport Expertise Routledge.
Accessed on: 12 Feb 2018
https://www.routledgehandbooks.-
com/doi/10.4324/9781315776675.ch31

7. Measuring Decisions

1. https://www.bostonglobe.com/2020/03/05/sports/how-sloan-sports-analytics-conference-grew-defunct-mit-class-really-big-deal/?event=event25
2. https://sports-biometrics-conference.com/
3. http://www.sloansportsconference.com/2020-conference/2020-research-paper-finalists-posters/

4. https://www.bostonglobe.com/2020/03/05/sports/how-sloan-sports-analytics-conference-grew-defunct-mit-class-really-big-deal/?event=event25

5. https://www.drucker.institute/thedx/measurement-myopia/

6. Doerr, John (2018). *Measure What Matters: How Google, Bono, and the Gates Foundation Rock the World with OKRs*. Penguin Publishing Group. p. 33. ISBN 9780525536239.

7. Lewis, Michael (2004). *Moneyball: The Art of Winning an Unfair Game*. W. W. Norton. ISBN 0393066231.

8. https://www.drucker.institute/thedx/measurement-myopia/

9. https://sabr.org/history/a-history-of-sabr

10. https://www.baseball-almanac.com/quotes/quosphn.shtml

11. https://baseballsavant.mlb.com/

12. Author written interview, Oct 4, 2017

13. Lowe, Zach, Bill Barnwell, Ben Lindbergh, and Brian Phillips, "Lights, Cameras, Revolution," Grantland, 2017, http://grantland.com/features/the-toronto-raptors-sportvu-cameras-nba-analytical-revolution/.

14. Author written interview, Oct 4, 2017

15. Author written interview, Oct 4, 2017

16. Author written interview, Oct 4, 2017

17. Author written interview, Oct 4, 2017

18. Author written interview, Oct 4, 2017

19. Author written interview, Oct 4, 2017

20. The section above was previously posted on the author's website: http://www.80percentmental.com/blog/2018/1/19/learning-from-ghosts-how-ai-and-machine-learning-are-changing-sports

21. https://www.statsperform.com/resource/player-tracking-deep-learning-innovations-lead-greater-interactions-data/

22. https://www.chicagomag.com/Chicago-Magazine/October-2018/Sports-Stats/

23. https://www.statsperform.com/resource/player-tracking-deep-learning-innovations-lead-greater-interactions-data/

24. https://tucson.com/sports/arizonawildcats/basketball/tell-me-why-spatial-technology-might-be-the-next-big/article_db13c850-299e-5821-ada1-4829ca4e42aa.html

25. https://tucson.com/sports/arizonawildcats/basketball/tell-me-why-spatial-technology-might-be-the-next-big/article_db13c850-299e-5821-ada1-4829ca4e42aa.html
26. https://sloanreview.mit.edu/audio/mapping-tom-bradys-brain/
27. https://sloanreview.mit.edu/audio/mapping-tom-bradys-brain/
28. http://www.sloansportsconference.com/wp-content/uploads/2019/02/DeepQB.pdf
29. https://sloanreview.mit.edu/audio/mapping-tom-bradys-brain/
30. https://sloanreview.mit.edu/audio/mapping-tom-bradys-brain/
31. https://www.theringer.com/2020/4/17/21224389/nfl-draft-quantifying-quarterback-evaluation

8. Improving Decisions

1. https://www.huffingtonpost.ca/entry/generation-alpha-after-gen-z_l_5d420ef4e4b0aca341181574
2. https://www.huffingtonpost.ca/entry/generation-alpha-after-gen-z_l_5d420ef4e4b0aca341181574
3. https://www.nytimes.com/2015/09/19/fashion/meet-alpha-the-next-next-generation.html
4. https://www.strategy-business.com/article/NBA-Commissioner-Adam-Silver-Has-a-Game-Plan
5. https://www.nielsen.com/wp-content/uploads/sites/3/2019/12/game-changer-gen-z-sports-report-2019.pdf
6. https://www.nytimes.com/interactive/2020/02/18/magazine/esports-business.html
7. https://www.huffingtonpost.ca/entry/generation-alpha-after-gen-z_l_5d420ef4e4b0aca341181574
8. Zaichkowsky, Leonard. The Playmaker's Advantage: How to Raise Your Mental Game to the Next Level. 2018 Gallery/Jeter Publishing. Kindle Edition.
9. Zaichkowsky, Leonard. The Playmaker's Advantage: How to Raise Your Mental Game to the Next Level . Gallery/Jeter Publishing. Kindle Edition.
10. https://www.discovermagazine.com/mind/screen-time-is-replacing-playtime-and-thats-changing-kids-brains

11. https://www.sciencedirect.com/science/article/abs/pii/S0360131514001869

12. https://www.popsci.com/article/gadgets/portal-2-improves-cognitive-skills-more-lumosity-does-study-finds/

13. https://www.popsci.com/article/gadgets/portal-2-improves-cognitive-skills-more-lumosity-does-study-finds/

14. https://www.nature.com/articles/nature01647

15. https://www.ted.com/talks/daphne_bavelier_your_brain_on_video_games/transcript

16. Bavelier D, Green CS. The Brain-Boosting Power of Video Games. Sci Am. 2016 Jul;315(1):26-31. doi: https://10.1038/scientificamerican0716-26. PMID: 27348376

17. https://www.sensearena.com/

18. https://gamesensesports.com/

19. https://www.ted.com/talks/daphne_bavelier_your_brain_on_video_games/transcript

20. Carlo Ancelotti. "Quiet Leadership: Winning Hearts, Minds and Matches.", 2016, Penguin Random House UK

21. https://www.nytimes.com/2020/10/16/sports/soccer/liverpool-everton-carlo-ancelotti.html?searchResultPosition=3

22. Carlo Ancelotti. "Quiet Leadership: Winning Hearts, Minds and Matches.", 2016, Penguin Random House UK

23. Carlo Ancelotti. "Quiet Leadership: Winning Hearts, Minds and Matches.", 2016, Penguin Random House UK

24. https://www.ukcoaching.org/resources/topics/tips/eight-recommendations-for-coaching-decision-making

25. Abdul-Jabbar, Kareem. Coach Wooden and Me: Our 50-Year Friendship On and Off the Court. Grand Central Publishing. Kindle Edition.